Transform
A rebel's guide for digital transformation

Gerry McGovern

Silver Beach Publishing

First edition

Published in 2016
Silver Beach Publishing
Silver Beach
Gormanston
Meath
Ireland
K32 YN40

ISBN: 978-1-78280-738-4 – Transform

Cover Design: Lisa Coffey
Editing: Rosilda Moreira Alves McGovern, Fionn McGovern
Reviews and comments: Mike Atyeo, Guy Stratermans
Typesetting and design: Anne Coffey
Indexing: Seán Moraghan (353 86 7397458)

www.digitaltransformationscore.com

www.customercarewords.com

ABOUT THE AUTHOR

Gerry McGovern has written six books on digital transformation and the online customer experience. He is the founder of Customer Carewords, a company that has developed a set of tools and methods to help large organizations improve online customer experience by identifying and optimizing their customers' top online tasks.

Gerry started his web career in 1994, and has spoken and consulted in more than 30 countries. His commercial clients include Microsoft, Cisco, NetApp, VMware, and IBM. He has also consulted with the European Union, the US, UK, Dutch, Canadian, Norwegian, and Irish governments.

@gerrymcgovern
gerry@customercarewords.com
www.customercarewords.com

To Rosilda

CONTENTS

CONTENTS

1
OPTIMISTS AND REBELS

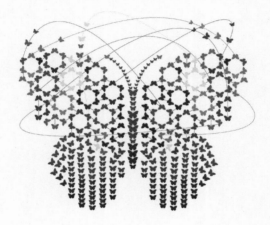

Optimists and Rebels

Are you an optimist? Are you a rebel? Do you think that because of digital technology, power is shifting away from organizations towards citizens and customers? Are you a digital change agent? Do you want to transform your organization? Then this book is here to help you.

Do you want to transform the complex into the simple? Do you like challenges and see yourself primarily as a problem solver? Are you the annoying person who constantly asks: "Why?" Are you empathetic? Do you like to listen, watch, observe? Are you also rational? Are you willing to go with the evidence and data, even when it goes against your gut instinct?

> Most organizations like to talk about customer-centricity, but they rarely practice what they preach.

Transform is for customer champions and advocates because the essence of digital transformation is about moving from organization-centric to customer-centric. Power has shifted. Customers are much more powerful today. Thus, becoming truly, obsessively customer-centric is the most radical, transformative thing you can do.

This is a book for those who are searching for a new model for how to fully embrace the opportunities that digital offers. Do you look at your organization and say: "Our model is broken. The way we do things around here, it's just not working anymore."

Transform is about a new customer-centric model of thinking and management. It offers a customer-centric philosophy and approach. It gives you the evidence for why the old model simply isn't working anymore. It gives you a new management model which is founded in customer outcomes.

If you've been doing this customer-centricity stuff for a while, then you'll know that your lot is not always an easy one. Yes, most organizations like to talk about customer-centricity, but they rarely practice what they preach. Because the old model of organization-centricity with its silos and its egos used to be much more comfortable and profitable. Until now.

The stuff in this book is risky—there's no point in pretending otherwise. It's about a new model. The old model—the old hierarchy—will not roll over easily. There will be resistance, and unfortunately the most dangerous element of that resistance is likely to come from senior management. Because old model senior management is over-rated, over-paid and underperforming when it comes to leading the necessary transformation that must occur.

I met David Shaw around 2009 when he was editor for the Scottish Enterprise website. (An organization focused on supporting Scottish entrepreneurs.) Like many other website managers, he was frustrated with his job. He told me about how different it was to his previous job as editor manager of Scottish Fishing Weekly, a very successful print magazine. When he was editor there, he was four days of the week on the road. He was out with the fishermen and only came into the office on Fridays. He knew his audience inside out and focused relentlessly on the issues that were important to them.

As editor of the Scottish Enterprise website, he spent five days a week in the office doing "digital" stuff and hardly ever met or communicated with a customer. He had become what I call a "put-it-upper" (derives from the Latin "put-it-uppo"). He launched stuff, published stuff, put stuff up on the website because someone somewhere else in the organization said to put it up. David knew that this was not the right thing to do. The website was growing fast and had lots of outdated information that nobody wanted to review or remove. But he didn't have the hard evidence because he wasn't in touch with his customers.

The customer champion has a very bright future to look forward to, though there are certainly risks involved.

I was in contact with David recently and he said to me this: "Still fighting the good fight! I've always been the troublemaking 'what about the customer' guy and must say it has been career limiting." Career limiting? Yes, up until now most customer champions had very little chance of progressing up the management hierarchy. But things are changing. The customer champion has a very bright future to look forward to, though there are certainly risks involved.

This is a time of revolution and revolutions are dangerous times. Many hierarchies hate the fact that customers have more power, and they resent those employees who are the voice of the customer. (The fact that, deep down, they know you're right doesn't mean they'll dislike you any less.) Many organizations simply do not have enough will to make the painful change from organization-centric to customer-centric. They will wither as the new model blossoms.

You will switch jobs a lot of times during your career and you'll switch brands even more as a customer. It's just the nature of digital: fluid, dynamic, rapidly evolving. So, you will need to be able to evaluate whether the organization that you are currently working with has the capacity or willingness to change. One of the best possible tests of digital readiness is "switchability". The more old-model the organization is the harder they try to make it for customers to switch. New model organizations empower customers with information and strive to make everything as simple as possible. So, one of the greatest things you can do in order to help the new model to thrive is to design the switches. Design the things that give control to the customer, that allow them to easily compare and switch, that allow them to connect, collaborate and share with their peers, that allow them to understand what they need to know in the fastest, simplest possible manner.

Transform gives you a new management model that is centered in the world of the customer, rather than the world of the organizational silo. Is your organization flexible, nimble and ready to adapt, or is it rigid, hierarchical and slow to change? Should you stay or should you go? And if it's somewhere in-between, as most organizations are, Transform will give you a method, a way of thinking, a model by which you can contribute to the digital transformation that must occur in order to be fit for survival in this new model.

2
TRANSFORMING A CULTURE

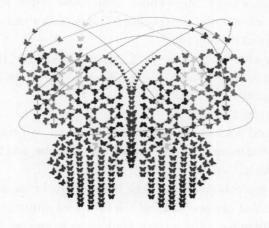

Transforming a Culture
The opportunity ahead

It's the best of times. It's the worst of times. Being customer-centric is the new motto. It's where every organization knows it must get to. But those who champion the customer are often seen as troublemakers. Why? Because if you're customer centric, then you're asking for content to be rewritten so that it will be shorter and easier to understand, for transparency in pricing and procedures, for simpler, more intuitive interfaces. All of this "making it easier for customers" makes it harder for your management and your colleagues. It's more work, more effort. They know you're doing the right thing but they don't like all the extra effort. This book is about changing that perception. It's about turning you from a rebel into a hero, or at the very least getting you much more respect and recognition. It's about giving you a model that allows

> Culture eats technology and strategy for breakfast.

your manager and your colleagues to see that their careers will become more successful the more customer-centric they become, and the more they support your efforts.

As a digital professional, your week is often equal measures optimism and frustration. You can see and feel the future all around you, but your organization is not moving fast enough. Sometimes it can even feel like things are going backwards. You struggle to find the key that will truly unlock a vibrant digital future. The key is culture because culture eats technology and strategy for breakfast.

There are many ways to become more customer-centric. The usability and customer experience professions are founded on such principles. I'm going to give you one method called Top Tasks. It's something I've developed over the last twenty years of working with organizations to make their websites more customer-centric. It's just one method—another tool in your toolbox—but I think it will be helpful to your efforts—and I have the evidence to prove it! Top Tasks Management has the following steps:

1. With clear and unambiguous data, identifying what really matters to your customers—their top tasks.
2. Measuring how able customers are to complete their top tasks and then

continuously improving these tasks based on these metrics.

3. Assembling teams around these tasks and making these teams responsible for customer task success. So, employees manage and are responsible for customer task outcomes, not organizational inputs.

A lot of this book, though, is going to be about culture and society, because that's where the game is truly at. What I have learned again and again is that you can change the technology and the website design, but if you don't change the culture, nothing important changes. I'm going to explore deeply the context within which digital transformation is occurring, because the first step in creating a new model culture is to understand the old model culture.

Much about our society and economy is broken today. Digital transformation offers us a grand opportunity to create a better society and economy that puts customers and citizens needs first—rather than the needs of the elites. I know there are huge challenges to achieving this more equitable society, but I am hugely optimistic, because I am absolutely certain that the organizations that will create the greatest value in the future will be those who are the most customer-centric.

Pioneers

The Irish have long made an art form out of being miserable. After all, it was an Irish man, Samuel Beckett, who said: "You must go on. I can't go on. I'll go on." When I was young, we were pretty poor and, yes, miserable. I lived on a small farm that wasn't even in the middle of nowhere. When everyone was gone to bed, I would sneak down to the kitchen

> You can't do this alone. You can – and will do it – with the right team, the right network.

to watch John Wayne and Clint Eastwood Westerns on our black and white TV, with a reception that seemed to be coming from Mars. I so envied those wagons as they rolled out towards new frontiers. "I'll never get that opportunity," I said miserably. I made myself a promise, though, that if I ever saw those wagons during my lifetime, I'd jump on.

In 1993, I came across the Web for the first time and instantly I saw those wagons rolling. And I jumped on. I've fallen off many, many times, but somehow I've managed to scramble back on. It's been an incredible trip. And it still is! What a privilege to be part of the emergence of this new online world. What a privilege to meet so many fascinating and passionate people along the way. Sure, there have been setbacks but that's the lot of pioneers. There's still so much promise, so much possibility. Online is in a state of revolution. It is about the rise of customer power. And the revolution is still in the early stages. Nobody said it was going to be easy. (At least, nobody I talked to.)

I can't tell you the amount of times that audiences have said to me over the years that I was "preaching to the choir." That they get it. It's just the "higher-ups" who don't get it. Well, it's time for the choir to start singing in a collective, multidisciplinary unison, because the choir has a lot more ability to make the change happen than it thinks it has. You can't do this alone. You can—and will do it—with the right team, the right network. And what do you have to do? Just change the culture.

Cultures can change: the story of Liberia and Ebola

Funerals are deep in the culture of a people. A Liberian funeral used to be a great affair. It was a celebration, with bands of trumpeters and drummers, and long processions, youngsters singing, the waving of open palms high above heads, a jubilation. Everyone went. All the locals, family members travelled long distances. The men in their best suits, the women in black outfits, children dressed in white. There might be soccer teams attending, local schools marching; an event, a big event. It could last for days, even weeks.

In preparation for the funeral, the body would be bathed, washed, rubbed and caressed by family members. There would be hugs and kisses of the dead. Death is a next stage of life, according to Liberian belief, a journey to the "Village of the Dead." The way the deceased are mourned and buried can impact what position they come to attain in the Village. If the ceremony is not carried out properly then the family may be in danger from an angered spirit, who can cause disease and harm.

Ebola struck on March 30, 2014. A dead body is more contagious than a living one. By September, the disease was growing exponentially and treatment centers were filling up the day they opened. Ebola was rampant. It was out of control. However, by May 2015, the WHO declared "Liberia free of Ebola virus transmission."

How did they do it? How did they change deep-seated cultural practices, many of which worked in direct opposition to combatting the spread of Ebola? It was by no means easy, as Liberia was in the process of recovering from a destructive 14 year Civil War that had killed over 200,000 people. Before Ebola struck, there were no more than 50 doctors for a population of 4.5 million. The best hospitals in Monrovia, the capital, didn't even have running water, let alone electricity or proper medical supplies.

Initial responses were often chaotic and corrupt. Clinics did not follow protocols, there was misdiagnosis, deep superstitions, wild rumors, infected healthcare workers kept working, donations were requested "to help the fight against Ebola" but merely ended up lining the pockets of the corrupt.

Three pillars of change began to emerge though:
1. Active community involvement. This was the most essential element. The local communities were given the tools and support to take back control of their own destinies and they did, changing their culture in the process.
2. Leadership. The Liberian government showed decisiveness and a willingness to make tough decisions.
3. International support. The wider network of the global community provided vital expertise, equipment and experienced professionals.

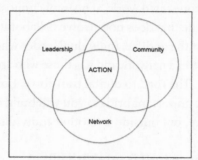

Optimal Action Framework

If we're to make change happen within the organization, the same three pillars must be used:
1. The network is the hub of change. Customers and partners drive digital transformation more than the organization itself. The organization

is led by the network, not the other way around. The customer is the spear point of change. The force is with the customer. This is the Age of the Customer.

2. The employee community must be fully engaged. They must be enabled to make the change happen. The employees are key. The "choir" needs to sing before management will listen.

3. Management—particularly senior management—must be seen to be embracing and encouraging the change.

> Digital transformation involves building bridges outside your peer group – your comfort zone.

Unfortunately, management is often the weakest link because to truly embrace digital transformation, management must give up a lot of the control that it was used to under the old model.

Real change will occur when these three pillars are supporting each other. So, how is that different from traditional old models of management, you might ask? It used to be that management led and that customers and employees were expected to follow. The Web has changed that power structure dynamic. Customers and employees have far more power today than they ever had— and they are beginning to exercise it.

In a complex, interconnected world, it is simply impossible to do anything substantial or worthwhile that does not involve collaboration across multiple disciplines. The myth of the godlike, individual leader who knows it all is less and less credible. We live in a network and it is those who are best at networking who will succeed most. The road to digital transformation involves building bridges—and the most important bridges you will build are not within your discipline or peer group, but outside it to other individuals and groups.

Hope replaces fear (once trust is established)

Lots of mistakes were made at the beginning of the Liberian struggle against Ebola. In complex, unpredictable worlds, mistakes are reality. Accept that you are going to make lots and lots of mistakes. Just make sure you develop a way to learn from your mistakes, adapt and refine and move on, constantly iterating.

At the beginning of the Liberian Ebola crisis, fear based messaging was often used, but this created a sense of paralysis, hopelessness and paranoia. The messaging had to change to one of hope and action: You can control your destiny. You can defeat this. Here's what you have to do. Don't design to control. Design to give control.

There is a lot of fear in society. People see how their income is stagnating, while the rich 1% is just getting richer. At a senior management level, many decisions are ruled by fear and ego. Robots stand on the horizon waiting to take over even more jobs. There is stress, overwork, a sense of being overwhelmed. Globally, 70% of employees are disengaged from their work. Something is badly broken. You need to fight fear with hope, because there is genuine reason for hope. If organizations become employee-centric and customer-centric, there is huge value to be gained.

To make the change happen, your colleagues must feel that there is a better place where they can get to. How will a customer-centric world be better than an organization-centric one? People must feel in control of their own destiny, they must feel able to do something. Hope can spring from purposeful work. Too many people do work that lacks purpose or real feedback today. In old model organizations, employees' careers are dependent, not on the quality of the work they do, but on how likeable they are, and how well they obey their managers. The stuff they produce (content, code, graphics, or whatever) seems to get sucked into a black hole. They never hear back about whether it worked or not, about what needs to be improved. The Top Tasks approach is about management based on constant feedback. Customers provide feedback. Employees make changes, and see the direct impact of their work makes it easier for customers. As customers see things getting simpler, they give more and better feedback.

Trust is a most precious, scarce resource

Building trust was vital to success in Liberia. Corruption was ever present, so getting people to trust the communication required huge transparency and extensive interactions with village chiefs, religious leaders, women's associations, youth groups, etc. The walls of the treatment centers were made of see-through plastic, so that families and friends could watch what was happening. This helped dispel fears and rumors.

There is a collapse of trust in institutions and leaders around the world today, as I will explain in more detail in later chapters. It will never return to the levels of blind trust that we used to have fifty years ago. This has huge implications for the digital designer, as we'll see later. Today, we trust in transparency, we trust in facts and evidence, so we must design for transparency. You build trust into your designs and content. How do you do that? You design for simplicity of use. That which is easy to use and understand, we trust. We distrust complexity.

> Design for simplicity of use. What is easy to use, we trust. We distrust complexity.

Organization culture must change

The wider, global network ultimately played a vital role in combating Ebola, but was initially found wanting. The pinnacle of organization-centric culture is senior management, and the change to a customer-centric culture will severely affect those who have authoritarian streaks, bountiful egos and mega wage packets. That is why you must be very careful in your transformative effort. Making your organization more customer-centric is a rebellious act against traditional hierarchy. You are walking a tightrope between empathy and ego. Most senior managers like to talk customer-centricity and collaboration but they don't want to be customer-centric.

The World Health Organization (WHO), which is responsible for managing global epidemics, was initially slow and inefficient in its response to the Ebola outbreak. "WHO does not have a culture of rapid decision-making and tends to adopt a reactive, rather than a proactive, approach to emergencies," an expert panel reported in 2015. "In the early stages of the Ebola crisis, messages were sent by experienced staff at headquarters and the Regional Office for Africa, including after deployments in the field, about the seriousness of the crisis. Either these did not reach senior leaders or senior leaders did not recognize their significance. WHO does not have an organizational culture that supports open and critical dialogue between senior leaders and staff or that permits risk-taking or critical approaches to decision-making," the report stated.

Sound familiar? Despite—or maybe because of—all these information management systems, senior managers are increasingly out-of-touch. This is an unfortunate reality in so many organizations today. Senior management often seems to live in a parallel bubble universe, making impossible promises and wanting to hear only positive stories about how these promises are being met. You need to play your part in bursting the bubble without the vengeance of management raining down on you. The actual experience of your customers is your spear point. If anything will burst the bubble and bring a true desire to become customer-centric, this will. Many in senior management are genuinely unaware of how horrible they have made things for their customers and employees. When they are shown evidence, it can be a real lightbulb moment.

Be careful, though. Avoid putting forward your opinion because your opinion versus a senior manager's gut instinct is not a battle you will win. Use data of customer experience to move things forward. Show how the customer is having a really bad experience. Keep talking about the customer.

The Ebola factsheet page from the WHO website became a classic example of the worst of office politics and organization-centric culture and silo-based thinking. This page was a critically important resource. It has had many millions of visitors since it was launched. Yet it was a real challenge to get this page reviewed and updated, according to Christopher Strebel, editor in chief of the WHO website.

The reason was that WHO was so focused on publishing new information about Ebola that it struggled to review and update essential content that was already published. It seemed that everybody within WHO wanted to publish something on Ebola, to show what they or their division was doing to combat the disease. WHO knew how important the factsheet page was, how it was infinitely more important than the vast majority of other pages on Ebola, but it too was paralyzed by old model organizational culture as it found itself caught up in a tsunami of internal publishing. It was caught up in that old, corrosive culture of organizational ego: "I am important. Therefore I publish a lot."

That is why as a first step in digital transformation you must establish the customer top tasks—what is really important to them. Unfortunately, what you will often discover as you go through the process of identifying top tasks is that what is most important to the customer is often least important to

Ebola factsheet page from the WHO website

the organization—and vice versa. Once you have identified the customer top tasks, you must measure them. How many customers are able to successfully complete these tasks? How long is it taking them? Show how they can't find basic facts. Show how they do find out-of-date information.

Measure use, not what you produce

Built into our old model DNA is the strong impulse to produce, to create, to publish, to own, to have, and to be seen to have. That's because we come from a physical world that is based on the laws of scarcity. Value is measured based on production and having lots of things. This is at the heart of organizational culture. It is alien to most organizations to continuously improve—to review, renew, and where appropriate, remove, that which already exists, particularly when it comes to content.

> **What is of most importance to the customer is often of least importance to the organization.**

There are two main reasons for this. Firstly, the organization feels it always has to show it is doing something new. Old model marketers, communicators, developers, designers are obsessed with the new, whether it is new customers, new events, new products, new features, new channels, new formats, new programs or new initiatives. They rarely see it as part of their job to focus on current customers, current programs, products, content, etc.

Secondly, in the old model things age, break down, degrade, fade away, get lost. Most physical stuff that is printed disappears over time, or as they used to say: "Today's news is tomorrow's fish 'n' chip paper". That print brochure or factsheet you published in 2010, where is it now? Most print ends up in history's dustbin.

Not so for digital. Unless the system crashes and there's no back-up, then digital stuff is going to stay around forever. If there is no process to renew or remove what is out-of-date content, redundant or simply no longer necessary, then all that old stuff will grow and grow and grow. Year in, year out it will become a larger percentage of the digital landscape. In other words, unless you maintain and continuously improve your digital environment, then the entire environment will naturally degrade. In a network, if you do nothing, things get worse. The US Department of Health had 200,000 pages on their website. They finally got around to deleting 150,000 of them that were old and out-of-date. Nobody noticed.

Your future will be more about continuously improving what you have created than creating new stuff. That's a big shift. You need to change habits. Your questions must be: "What can I remove? What can I improve?" Not: "What can I add? What can I create?" I know that management wants you to produce, not maintain. Real work—real value in the old model—is when you create something new, not when you improve or delete something. You are rewarded and measured by what you produce—a traditional input-based metric that often ends up rewarding worst practice in a digital world.

We must change the metrics. We must change the model. You need metrics that are focused on how customers find and use what your organization produces. When you measure these customer outcomes, you will notice the negative impact of the old and outdated. In a network, you need outcome-based metrics that focus on how people use things. Traditional metrics of production merely measure what happens within the organizational silo.

In October 2014, I searched for "latest Ebola death figures" on the WHO website. The first search result was from April 2nd, the second result was from April 1st, the third result was from August 4th and the fourth result was from April 22nd. Isn't that shocking? Research on how people use search engines show that over 60% will click within the first three search results. Are these out-of-date search results acceptable? Of course, not. But most organizations do not measure findability (the outcome). They just measure the input (the search engine itself and the content that is indexed). This culture must change.

When in August 2015, I searched for "ebola death toll by country" on the WHO website, I got the following results.

We must move from managing organizational inputs to managing customer outcomes.

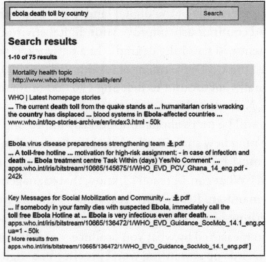

WHO search results for "ebola death toll by country"

None of the results were particularly useful. In fact, on the first page of search results 8 out of 10 of the results were PDFs. Nothing better illustrates an organization-centric, old model culture than the proliferation of PDFs on a website because one thing is for sure: digitizing print documents is not digital transformation.

When I did the exact same search in Google, I got the results shown on the following page.

This is the digital future. We don't want to search. We want to find an answer quickly. What is the purpose of the WHO website when Google gives answers more quickly and easily? Wikipedia is becoming as popular as WHO

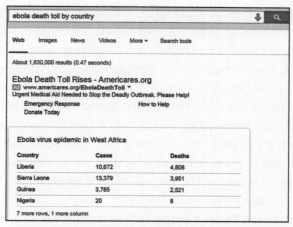

Google search results for "ebola death toll by country"

as a source of health information. Increasingly, if traditional organizations cannot overcome their organization-centric cultures, so as to professionally manage and maintain their own information, they will be supplanted by more efficient network operators. If WHO can't become useful on the Web, then someone else will do its job for it.

Endlessly flexible, evolving cultures

We'll never get our organization to change, I often hear the beaten-down web professional say. They're too fixed in their ways. But it only takes one generation for something to seem like it was there forever. Things are a lot more fluid than you might think.

"Funerals can confuse a visitor to Monrovia, the capital of Liberia," Stanley Meisler wrote for The Atlantic Monthly in 1973. "Is he on the western coast of Africa or in New Orleans?" Meisler described how the "the big brass band marches down Broad Street on a hot Sunday afternoon, playing rollicking hymns … It shouldn't be a shock to come across a New Orleans funeral an ocean away in West Africa, but it is. A few moments' reflection, however, produces the obvious logic for it all. Slaves from Africa, with their traditions of joyous mourning, turned the sedate white man's funeral into a black man's jazzy funeral in Louisiana. Freed slaves then carried it back to Africa."

Things have always been changing and intermixing; we just don't notice sometimes. Culture is always changing, just sometimes slowly enough for most to think everything is remaining the same. Digital is much faster than physical. It changes much more rapidly and it will drag culture along whether it likes it or not. Those organizations that can't change at the speed of digital will wilt away in the network.

Today and tomorrow and forever more, we can't avoid seeing the change, and willing—or unwilling—being part of that change, because it's all speeding up. It's all at a frenetic pace now. Nothing is ever finished. Nothing is ever over anymore. There is no definitive anything, no fundamental truths, no absolute answers. We have entered an age of great uncertainty and we're just going to have to adapt—and we will!

There is no guarantee of a happy future for Liberia. Throughout 2015, Liberia had isolated incidents of Ebola. The system must be ever vigilant. It's actually much easier to change back to old model organizational culture because old model is tribal culture, and this is the deepest and oldest culture of all. Organizations are just another type of tribe, and it is always more comfortable to look inwards; comfortable but not safe.

Are you thinking that in some ways it was easier for Liberia to change because they faced an existential crisis, an extinction event? They had to act. They felt they had no choice. There are always choices. To do nothing is a choice. To move slowly is a choice.

For old model organizations, the extinction event is the Web.

We are living in an insecure and complex world where random events with major consequences are happening with increasing frequency. We must get used to it because insecurity and complexity is only going to increase.

For traditional organizations, and traditional, rigid minds, the extinction event has, in fact, already happened.

It's called The Web.

References

Beckett, S. *Three Novels: Molloy, Malone Dies, The Unnamable,* Grove Press, New York, 1955

Meisler, S. *Liberia,* The Atlantic Monthly, Mar. 1973
http://www.theatlantic.com/past/docs/issues/73mar/meisler.htm

World Health Organization. *The Ebola outbreak in Liberia is over,* WHO, May 2015
http://www.who.int/mediacentre/news/statements/2015/liberia-ends-ebola/en/

3
TRANSFORMING
ORGANIZATIONAL CULTURE

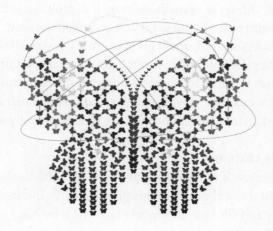

Transforming Organizational Culture
It is your opportunity

This is a revolution and transformation that is primarily being driven from the outside by customers, or from the bottom or middle of organizations, not from the top. It is a revolution of employees and customers. Yes, leadership matters but like in Liberia, the broader networks are the crucial drivers. Everything is connected. Getting to a new model culture will take years and the efforts of every unit in your organization. It will be a massive collaborative effort. It has to start somewhere.

The transformation begins not so much by thinking outside the box / silo, but by linking the boxes, by reaching out and finding others who want to be part of the transformation. The old model was a hierarchy full of silos and egos. Digital culture is network culture. It is multidisciplinary culture. Don't wait for your leadership to get it and then lead the way.

Lead your leadership. Help them get it, because it is you who see the future far better than they do. Leadership is often disconnected, set in its ways, and out-of-touch when it comes to understanding the opportunities and threats that we face. But we cannot move forward without senior management. The challenge is to educate them and bring them enthusiastically along.

Empathy for the customer

Customer experience is the spear point of change. The hardest thing is to feel for others. To think about other people's needs. To live in other people's shoes. Hierarchy and silos are all about tribes. The tribe has a powerful pull. It is comforting and ego-rewarding. Your group, your peers, your design, your content, your code.

To reach out and see the world from outside-in goes against gut instinct. That's the hardest skill. And it is the most essential one because the customer has become so much more powerful. Because if you don't focus relentlessly on the customer, they will leave. If you don't focus relentlessly on the employee, they will leave. And if they can't leave because you're a government or some sort of monopoly, they will refuse to use or read whatever it is you have created. They'll call you on the phone if they have to. Or they'll fill in the form with lots of mistakes.

One way or another they will find a way to rebel and make your life difficult. Everyone will get frustrated and annoyed. Value and opportunity will be lost for everyone. The customer has radically changed and we must change with the customer.

Focus on customer outcomes

We must change how we measure things and how we reward organizational behavior. Otherwise, nothing will really change. We may have one foot in the new model but practically all our management metrics measure old model inputs. We measure the production—the more of it the better—of things, whether they be

> **Opinion and gut instinct are relics of old model thinking.**

products, projects, content or code. We measure websites and webpages and apps. How many did we launch? How much did we create?

Wrong metrics! New model metrics measure customer outcomes. They measure consumption, impact. What happened? What was the customer able to do? How long did it take them? How easy was it for them? Did they leave with the wrong answer? We must move to outcome-based consumption metrics.

Use evidence, use Big and Little Data

Opinion and gut instinct will slowly be reshaped as evidence and data grows. Digital leaves a record that can be analyzed. At every step of the transformative process, you must show it, prove it, do it. What's Big Data except evidence of what happened, what people did, when they did it?

The best way to transform an organization to a new model culture is by using the Web as a laboratory of human behavior, where you are constantly testing and evolving hypotheses. You use evidence of what people actually do, not what they say they do. You test and test again and test again. If we do it the old way, show the results you get. If we do it the new way, show how you get much better results. Move forward with evidence. The path to the new model is paved with evidence of what your customers and employees are actually doing. Leadership from below can only succeed if it is driven by the evidence of what customers are doing.

The Top Tasks approach, which will be explained in later chapters, is a model of continuous improvement that, first and foremost, establishes what is most and least important to customers. It is about managing ongoing customer use. You manage the task, not the channel, not the format, not the content, not the code. You do this based on constant feedback from your customers. This feedback is the most valuable thing you can get. Thus, it's vital that you design and evolve within the environment of the customer. That means going live with the website or app as quickly as possible.

Digital is the never-ending experiment. The longer you keep it inside the silo, the less chance it has of success. Connect it up, let it loose. Get it out into the customer ecosystem and evolve it based on use. Don't build to last. Build to change. Find a product, or a section for a product, an area, a small place within the larger organization. Launch the new model and gather data. Test and refine, test and refine, test and refine. The new model will grow and over time replace the old model.

Digital Transformation Score

A giant meteorite was the extinction event for the dinosaurs. The Web is the digital extinction event for old-model organizational dinosaurs. The Web extinction event smashed all those old certainties. The organizational dinosaurs are not all dead by any means, but their future is far from bright. Unless they can find it within themselves to transform.

Organizations are not healthy. Whereas people's life expectancy has

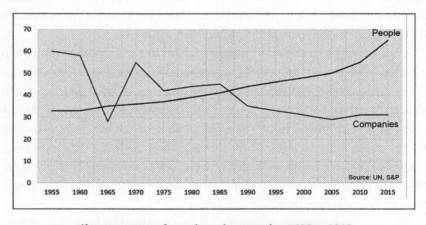

Life expectancy of people and companies: 1955 to 2015

gradually increased over the last sixty years, organizational life expectancy has halved. The preceding chart, compiled from UN and S&P data, might in fact be an overly rosy picture from a company perspective. Professor Richard Foster from Yale University estimated that in 2015 life expectancy of companies had dropped to 15 years, a 50-year decline on what they had been in the 1920s. Today's rate of change "is at a faster pace than ever", he told the BBC.

> You never change things by fighting the existing reality. Create a new model.

"Bureaucracies are honed by the past and almost never can they deal with the future," biologist Leroy Hood has stated. So, what do we do? We must create a new model, as Richard Buckminster Fuller stated: "You never change things by fighting the existing reality. To change something, build a new model that makes the existing model obsolete." The new model puts the customer at the center. It organizes around the customer and measures success, first and foremost—based on customer success.

This change of model from organization-centric to customer-centric will not be easy. "Growth creates interdependencies, interdependencies create conflicting constraints, and conflicting constraints create slow decision making and, ultimately, bureaucratic gridlock," Eric D. Beinhocker writes in his book, The Origin of Wealth. "The politics of organizations are such that local pain in particular groups or departments is often sufficient to prevent the organization from moving to a new state, even if that state is more globally fit … The virtual nonexistence of excellence that lasts multiple decades (again, less than 0.5 percent), and the extreme rarity of repeated excellence (again, 1 percent), brings us to a brutal truth about most companies. Markets are highly dynamic, but the vast majority of companies are not."

One thing is for sure. In the world digital is building, you will switch jobs many times during your career—and you will likely switch careers many times too. You need to know if your organization is a new model one—or at least if it has the potential to become one. Otherwise, you need to move to an organization that wants to be part of the future. Over the years, through feedback and research, I've developed a list of the core characteristics of new and old model organizations.

Score your organization by placing a 1 next to the factor that best reflects how you feel about it. *(For an online version, visit www.digitaltransformationscore.com)*

Score	Pre-Transformation	Score	Post-Transformation
	Doesn't care about me		Cares about me
	Doesn't support me when I have a problem		Supports me when I have a problem
	Doesn't protect my personal information		Protects my personal information
	Slow, reactive, imitator		Flexible, proactive, innovator
	Living in the past, resists change		Forward-looking, embraces change
	Disjointed experience		Integrated, seamless experience
	Makes it slow and hard for me to do things		Allows me to do things quickly and easily
	Getting more complicated		Continuously improving, simplifying
	Poor quality information and tools		Gives me the right information and tools
	Untrustworthy		Trustworthy
	Selfish, only interested in itself		Responsible, contributes to a better world
	Loves jargon, not open or transparent		Uses plain language, open, transparent

Digital Transformation Score

References

Beinhocker, E. *The Origin of Wealth: The Radical Remaking of Economics and What it Means for Business and Society*, Harvard Business Review Press, Aug. 2007

Boag, P. *Digital Adaptation*, Smashing Magazine GmbH, Germany, 2014

Gittleson, K. *Can a Company Live Forever?* BBC, Jan. 2012
http://www.bbc.com/news/business-16611040

4
GOLDEN AGE OF DIGITAL DESIGNERS

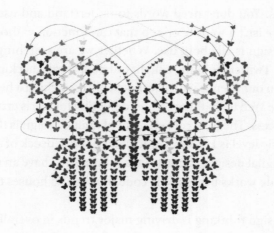

Golden Age of Digital Designers
Digital design is design for use

It's never been a better time to be a digital designer. But what do we mean by a "digital designer"? Initially, digital design was strongly linked with visual design. The visual look is an important element of digital design, but it is not the most important. The Web is primarily a functional, word-driven environment—whether we are talking about search or navigation—and it is the design / use of the right words that is a key pillar of digital design. Think of the most iconic of all digital designs: the search engine—it runs on words. Or think of how useful Facebook or Amazon would be without words. You don't need words to understand and use a hammer or chair, but there isn't a website or app that can function without words.

Design for use. We come to the Web to do things.

Digital design is all about use. Whether we are searching with Google, tweeting with Twitter, booking a flight or hotel room, checking the weather, checking up on our friends with Facebook, or researching a health symptom, we come to the Web to do things. Thus, designing for use is crucial to a digital designer's success. The final core element of digital design is the code, which at its most basic level is HTML. Good code is the bedrock of all great digital design, and digital designers must—at a minimum—have an understanding of how the code works because the code frames and houses the design.

Digital design thinking is driving major trends in overall design:

1. A move away from aesthetics/visuals which has dominated much of design over the last 30 years. As the great product designer, James Dyson has stated: "Styling for its own sake is a lazy 20th-Century conceit." And as Steve Jobs has stated: "Design is not just what it looks like and feels like. Design is how it works."

2. A move away from the programming and code to the interface. In early digital design, once the thing had been programmed and technically worked, it was launched. There was hardly any consideration given to making it easy to use. Basically, people were expected to learn how to use it. This sort of thinking has particularly dominated within traditional IT and enterprise design. It is being replaced by a greater focus on use and

simplicity. The "product" is now becoming the interface, not the code.

3. A holistic "experience" approach to design. Great digital design is co-designed with the customer and is focused not on any one element of the design (graphics, code, content) but rather on the experience of the customer using the design. It asks crucial questions: How easy is this to do? How fast is this to do?

4. A move away from fixed to flexible design. Traditional designers are used to controlling every element of the design. Digital designers come up with an adaptable, flexible system that fits into people's lives. Digital designs are designed to work whether you are using a smartphone, a tablet, laptop or desktop. The best digital design gives you the controls. You can search, compare, process, calculate, zoom, expand. Digital design is much more about giving you control than controlling you.

If you track terms such as "information architecture", "user interface" and "usability" in Google Trends between 2004 and 2015, you will notice a significant decline. These are digital design elements or disciplines or components. They are focused on the designers and how the designer designs. During the same period, you will notice a significant rise in searches for terms like "user experience", "customer experience" and "design thinking". These terms are focused on the outcomes, the customers' experience of and use of the design. We are shifting from a focus on design inputs to customer outcomes and experiences.

We'll never have enough designers!

If there is one department that you would expect to be super happy about the digital revolution, it would be Information Technology (IT). Yet as the digital world—which is essentially a technological world—explodes, the role and importance of traditional IT continues to decline.

Part of the reason is that IT was been wedded to a culture that is obsessed with the technology itself, rather than its use. Traditional IT became devoid of human interaction and feedback. The more you separate the creation of the thing from the use of the thing, the more you encourage complexity to grow. "The only business unit not interacting with customers is IT," Ventana Research stated in 2015. Think about that. The department that creates the things that the rest of us are supposed to use never interacts with us.

Up until quite recently, IT has been a hermetically-sealed world that perfectly excluded the employee or customer. The people who commissioned IT systems were never the ones who would actually use them. That is why—particularly in the enterprise—we have the torture chambers to be found under the label "Tools & Systems."

This is all changing, and at a very rapid pace, though it has a long way to go. If a modern company has customer experience at its heart, then roughly one in ten employees will be designers, according to Andreas Hauser, Global Head of Design for SAP. In a typical software vendor, roughly one in every 100 employees will be a designer. In a typical IT organization, roughly one in every 1,000 employees will be a designer.

> The key characteristic of the digital designer is empathy.

So, we need millions more designers! We need more writers who can work well with words in the content, the information architecture and interfaces. We need more visual designers. And we need lots and lots of customer experience designers. This is an absolutely wonderful age to be a digital designer!

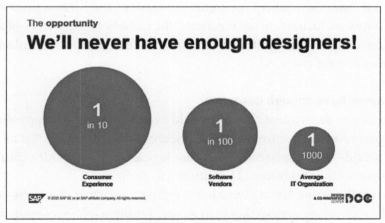

The opportunity
We'll never have enough designers!

1 in 10
Consumer Experience

1 in 100
Software Vendors

1 1000
Average IT Organization

SAP ratio of digital designers in organizations

Because great design pays. Customers and employees are simply refusing to use clunky, non-designed systems. The Design Management Institute estimated that design-led companies have outperformed the S&P by 228% between 2003 and 2013.

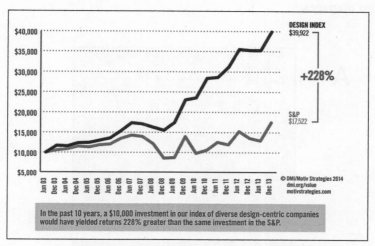

Design-led company S&P performance: 2003-2013

What is the key characteristic digital designers need? Empathy for the customer. Design has always been a war between ego and empathy. Today, more than ever, we need those who can imagine what it's like to be on the other side of the screen, because the irony is that digital touchpoints are separation points. They act as walls between the organization and the customer. So, a digital designer must have an intimate understanding of the customer. They must be able to imagine how a newbie feels when at a website or using a product for the first time. They must be obsessive about saving 1 second for the customer because they know that the empowered customer is ruthless about their time. There is no greater sin in the new model than wasting a customers' time. Empathy is such a rare and powerful skill and you develop it like you develop any skill. You practice, practice, practice. And practice comes from watching, observing, thinking about your customer. Every day. Every single work day you should be thinking about, observing and understanding your customer.

Don't trust your gut
SIMS is a hugely popular simulation game that allows you to create your

own town, your own virtual world. It wanted to improve sign-up for optional registration for those who had purchased the game. It tested the following two sign up pages.

A

B

One of these pages was 40 percent more successful at getting people to register. Now, if it was 0.4% better, that would be significant. If it was a 4% better that would be very significant, but 40% is absolutely huge. Trust your instinct. Which page was 40% more successful at getting people to register? A or B?

Did you choose B? I have asked thousands of web professionals at hundreds of conferences this question, and like clockwork 80% of them chose B. When this case study was published on Which Test Won, 80% of readers also chose B. Thus, in the web community, it's a no brainer, B is the best page.

Version A was 40% more successful.

That's worrying, but it's not surprising. And it's by no way an exception. I have used many other tests over the years where the design "experts" get it totally wrong. I chose A. I got it wrong too. It's not about who is right and who is wrong. Don't get into that debate. Test. Get evidence.

The brain works very differently when you look at something compared to when you use something. You must get evidence of what the customer actually does, not what you think they do, not what they think they do. As complexity increases, things become more counter-intuitive.

This is the golden age of decision-makers who make decisions using evidence of what customers are actually doing. We have the coming together of two big trends—customer experience and Big Data—to create a new design environment that is both empathetic and analytic. This golden age can't happen too soon because we have a new type of customer out there who has never been more demanding. They want convenience, control, and simplicity. And they want it now.

References

Hauser, A. *UX STRAT Europe, Andreas Hauser: Convincing IT and Business to Value Design,* June 2015
http://www.slideshare.net/UXSTRAT/convincing-it-and-business-to-value-design

Dimbleby, R. *The Richard Dimbleby Lecture - Engineering the Difference by James Dyson,* Sept. 2004
http://www.bbc.co.uk/pressoffice/pressreleases/stories/2004/12_december/09/dyson.shtml

Ventana Research. *In the Digital Economy, the Customer Experience is Critical,* Apr. 2015
http://www.ventanaresearch.com/blog/commentblog.aspx?id=4786

Walker, R. *The Guts of a New Machine,* The New York Times, Nov. 2003
http://www.nytimes.com/2003/11/30/magazine/30IPOD

5
DICTATORSHIP OF THE CUSTOMER

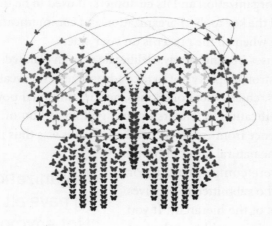

Dictatorship of the Customer
Rise of customer power

They say in marketing that the customer is king. The customer was never treated as much of a king, though. The customer was expected to be a good consumer and to buy what marketing and advertising told them to buy. The employee was expected to be a good and loyal worker and to do what their bosses and the communications department told them. And all was good from an organization-centric point of view, because organizations had pretty much all the power.

Unequal relationships inevitably lead to abuse. For a long time, there has been an unequal relationship between management and employees, and between the organization and its customers. It used to be that management controlled all the key tools of organization and communication. It's hard not to be abusive when all the power is on your side.

These abuses were not always deliberate or even planned. It is simply very hard for the stronger party not to take advantage of the weaker one. History is about gods, chiefs, dictators, kings, and institutional power. Its script is about the deification of leadership and godlike vision of "great men". To expect deference from employees and customers was thus normal practice. It reflected the natural order of things.

There were compensations for employees who submitted themselves to the wishes of the hierarchy. If you did what you were told and showed appropriate deference then you had a

Organizations used to have all the power. Not anymore.

reasonable chance of lifelong employment. If you were male and had talent and ambition you might even become king one day, or at least a prince.

Many organizations were benevolent dictatorships. They treated customers reasonably well. But, in general, unless there was strong competition, customers were exploited. Ironically, the most loyal customers tended to be treated the worst. The potential customer was king—as long as they were "potential"— and was promised everything, while the loyal customer was used as a "cash cow", milked for heavy profit.

The arrival of the Web was an extinction event for that old model. The Web is a mega-organization of customers. It makes widely available to employees and customers a flood of information and a vibrant network and set of tools within which to organize. Suddenly, employees and customers were no longer so dependent on traditional brands and organizations. They have Google, Facebook, Twitter, etc.

We are thus seeing a rebalancing—an equalizing—of the relationship between management, employees and customers. It's a very good thing because in balanced relationships, where each party has roughly equal power, there is a chance for real respect and genuine trust. We have the foundations for developing more robust relationships based on transparency and honesty. What could be more fertile ground on which to build loyalty and sustainable business models?

Being customer-centric

I remember one afternoon that I sat in an almost empty Starbucks café. At the next table, a Starbucks regional manager was doing reviews with staff.

"You've got a problem," he said in a low voice to one of them. "I'm getting reports that you're handing out lattes that are not filled up to the top. Why is that? Did you not want to hand it back to your colleague? Did you think they wouldn't be your friend anymore if you were seen to be annoying them?"

The conversation went back and forth but the manager kept stressing that the customer must be the absolute focus. Your fellow employees are NOT the customer, he stressed. Focus outwards, not inwards. This is service thinking. This is outcome-based management. This is customer-centric thinking, and outside the service industry, it is rare. But, of course, we're all in service now.

Service cultures can make for challenging workplaces (as anyone who has worked in Amazon will surely attest). Many employees seek a comfortable life with as little hassle as possible. In traditional, non-service-oriented organizations,

It's harder to develop empathy in a digital world.

one way to make your life as a worker easy is to ignore the customer. Make them fit into your schedule, learn your lingo, your processes, your logic, your way of doing things.

"It's kind of arrogant to think the only reason people exist is to use what you built," Facebook's director of product design, Margaret Gould Stewart has stated. But that is exactly the way it used to be. Many in traditional IT felt that the customer and employee should feel honored to read the manual—which they couldn't understand anyway—so as to use the technology they were privileged to be allowed to use. That's how it used to be. That's definitely not how it is now.

The challenge is that as we need to become more empathetic, the opportunities to develop empathy are declining. It is easiest to develop empathy when you are physically with someone. However, when someone is lost on your website or confused by your app, you don't see them. You are removed from their world, and that makes it harder to develop empathy for them. They're just a "user".

Jack Dorsey, creator of Twitter and founder and CEO of Square, has stated that, "It's time for our industry and discipline to reconsider the word "user". We speak about "user-centric design", "user benefit", "user experience", "active users", and even "usernames." While the intent is to consider people first, the result is a massive abstraction away from real problems people feel on a daily basis. From this moment forward, let's stop distancing ourselves from the people that choose our products over our competitors. We don't have users, we have customers, we earn. They deserve our utmost respect, focus, and service." (What does the drug and the Web industry have in common? Users, traffic and HITS.)

Digital touchpoints are oxymorons. They close down human-to-human interactions between the organization and the customer. The only things being touched are screens. So, in an age when the customer has never been more powerful, cynical and impatient, we have never had less opportunities to develop empathy for and understanding of our customers.

That's your job! There's nothing more important you can do. Nothing. You must be the voice and the champion of the customer within your organization. You must find every opportunity you can to show the actual experience of your customers to as many employees and management as you can. (The Task Performance Indicator, which will be described later in this book, is a method that helps you do exactly that.)

You will be the most empathetic professional around, knowing and understanding your customers' needs and how they behave in an online world better than they do themselves. You'll know exactly their top tasks and how to make them more findable and doable, and you'll know their tiny tasks and how to make sure these don't get in the way of the top tasks. And here's the first step in developing empathy: stop calling them "users". Call them customers, people, students, nurses, engineers, employees. Humanize them. Give them human names. Empathize with them.

> Organizations used to research customers. Now customers research organizations.

Loyalty is for suckers

Did I say that the customer is a dictator these days? The organization used to research the customer. Now, the customer researches the organization. They love the power a good search engine gives them. They love to review and give their opinion, knowing that social media is their megaphone and connector. This demanding, impatient and skeptical customer will become increasingly hard to serve and keep happy.

It won't be easy to be seen as the customer champion. You'll be adding to the workload of your fellow employees because the customer will demand that you make things incredibly simple and convenient. That means that you will have to go to your co-workers and ask them to make their work lives more complex and less convenient. And being a customer champion in an old model organization nearly always means that you will be in conflict with senior management objectives trying to push sales to potential customers at all costs, and exploit and overcharge current customers as much as possible.

Your future will be built on making life easier for current customers because that's where the true value of organizations lies.

- A 5% increase in customer retention produces more than a 25% increase in profit." (Fred Reichheld)
- 80% of future revenue for brands will come from just 20% of the existing customer base. (Gartner)
- It costs retail banks as much as six times more to attract a new customer than it does to retain an existing one. (Ernst and Young)
- Typically, it takes more than 3.5 years for a telecom company to break even on its subscriber acquisition cost. However, the average customer stays only about two years. (Ovum)

Why are loyal customers more valuable than potential customers?
- They buy more.
- The operating cost to manage a loyal customer tends to go down over time.
- Loyal customers tend to refer other customers. Loyal customers are the best possible social media strategy.
- A recommendation from a current customer is one of the few things that potential customers still trust.
- Current customers are often willing to pay a premium to do business with you because they are familiar and comfortable with you, and they don't want the hassle of switching.

And, boy, do they end up paying a premium! For decades, many brands have taken their loyal customers' for granted. Not just that. They have actively exploited these loyal customers' willingness to pay a premium, and have milked them for all they were worth. For example, many loyalty programs are deliberately designed to make customers less price sensitive by the use of emotional gimmicks. In other words, many loyalty programs are designed to overcharge the most loyal customers. As a senior executive once said to me: "If you get a gift out of the blue from us, then you can be certain we are absolutely creaming you for profits." At the same time, organizations have chased and chased

The old model has nearly always exploited the loyal customer.

potential customers, promising them everything under the sun. $40 billion is spent on digital advertising in the US on an annual basis, while between $2 and $5 billion is spent on designing services, according to Chris Risdon of Adaptive Path.

Because of the Web, more and more customers are finding out that they're being exploited and ripped off. They're not happy. Loyalty and trust, as we will see in later chapters, are nose-diving. In 2013, for example, Accenture found that customer switching costs companies almost $6 trillion every year, and every year more switch.

Organize around the customer

We have a department of selling to the customer, a department of marketing to the customer, a department of communicating at the customer. We have a department of support for dealing with customer complaints.

None of these departments really care about the customer, with the possible exception of the support department, but then support has very little prestige within an old model organization. Unless you're a company called Slack. In 2015, I had the pleasure of hearing Matt Haughey speak at An Event Apart conference. Matt is a real pioneer in the web industry. He is currently working with Slack to help their customers. Slack is a company that is revolutionizing the digital workplace. When I heard Matt talk about Slack at An Event Apart, my first thoughts were: "Can't be possible! Do companies like this actually exist!?" Matt explained that "customer experience is the second biggest group employed at Slack," and that the foundation of customer experience is good support.

- Every new employee does at least two full days of working the support queue.
- Designers and engineers do two hours per week of support, forever.
- All our support stuff is integrated into Slack, so you can see every ticket ever, review answers, etc.
- A weekly summary of support is sent on Monday mornings about the previous week in our general channel (which is very low traffic, announcements only).

Slack is a company that genuinely invests in the customer experience. And it pays. "Slack stands on the precipice of product mega-fame," Seth Stevenson wrote for the Wall Street Journal in November 2015. "There's a decent chance you haven't heard of it yet, and it sounds almost banal in description: software that helps groups of co-workers exchange instant messages and swap electronic files. Yet Slack is, by some estimates, the fastest-growing business application of all time."

Slack is a company where the desire to really help the customer is in the DNA of every employee. It is not just some phony marketing, advertising, PR communications propaganda about how "we care". Crazy as it sounds, Slack actually does care about its current customers. And because they treat their customers incredibly well, they're doing incredibly well.

Back in the old model organization, the customer champion—if there even is one—is a lonely, isolated voice, constantly trying to defend the interests of the customer. It's hard to be a customer champion when other departments have targets to meet that involve exploiting and annoying customers.

This is your challenge if you see fit to take it on. It is full of the amazing potential that always exists when one model dies and a new one in born. These sorts of times don't come often—most probably it is a once in a lifetime occurrence—when someone not in a senior management position can make a big, big difference. But it is fraught with danger and threats, as is always the case too. Because the old

The ego is rampant in the old model organization.

model organization won't die easily. It can linger on for quite a while, and become all the more vicious in its death spasms.

I remember once sitting in on a presentation where a bunch of marketers were presenting new product ideas and programs. Almost in unison, they said to the web manager: "And we'll be coming to you to get a banner on the homepage." The homepage was a cluttered mess and research showed that customers hated it. Most of the week for the web manager was spent fighting off requests for banners and other marketing and management ego fluff.

This website had a huge carousel for its banners. The web manager readily admitted that it was useless, that in fact it was counterproductive and was losing sales. But he said that the reason they had it was to keep marketing and management ego at bay. He called it the "Carousel of Egos". "They like interactive things and they like being on the homepage," he said. "Things that move and are flashy and that dominate the page they think will dominate the attention of the customer. They like to think they're in control of the message. And you can essentially deal with 5 ego requests in the one space with a carousel. So even though hardly anyone looks at it or clicks on it, it does keep our managers happy."

This old model of organization-centricity and ego is still rampant today, and this is what you have to deal with. You might decide to give the homepage to the Egos because that a battle you know you're not going to win. And anyway, you know that every year the homepage gets less and less visits as customers find what they want through Google and external links.

So, it's very unlikely you can introduce the new customer centric model on the homepage. You find somewhere else, like a particular product page, or maybe in support. You may have to wait. You may require more evidence of how treating customers well is the best possible business model. Keep collecting that evidence. Be patient because the movement of history is on your side. The world of the old model organizations is burning as trust collapses.

References

Reichheld F. & Schefter P. *The Economics of E-Loyalty,* Harvard Business School, Oct. 2000
http://hbswk.hbs.edu/archive/1590.html

Lawrence, A. *Five Customer Retention Tips for Entrepreneurs,* Forbes, Nov. 2012
http://www.forbes.com/sites/alexlawrence/2012/11/01/five-customer-retention-tips-for-entrepreneurs/#67a72ced17b0

Ernst and Young. *Understanding Customer Behavior in Retail Banking. The Impact of Credit Crisis across Europe*, Feb. 2010
http://www.ey.com/Publication/vwLUAssets/Understanding_customer_behavior_in_retail_banking_-_February_2010/$FILE/EY_Understanding_customer_behavior_in_retail_banking_-_February_2010.pdf

Cary, C. *Telcos Must Turn Big Data into Smart Data to Manage Customer Churn and Loyalty,* Aug. 2015
http://www.ovum.com/press_releases/telcos-must-turn-big-data-into-smart-data-to-manage-customer-churn-and-loyalty/

Dorsey, J. *Let's Reconsider Our "Users",* 2013
http://jacks.tumblr.com/post/33785796042/lets-reconsider-our-users

O'Reilly, L. *Facebook: We Don't Call Them 'Users' Any More, We Call Them 'People',* Business Insider UK, Dec. 2014
http://uk.businessinsider.com/facebook-says-it-has-dropped-the-term-users-and-has-an-empathy-team-2014-12?r=US&IR=T

Stevenson, S. *Stewart Butterfield, Email Killer,* WSJ Magazine, Nov. 2015
http://www.wsj.com/articles/slack-ceo-stewart-butterfield-on-changing-the-way-we-work-1446689564

6
COLLAPSE OF TRUST

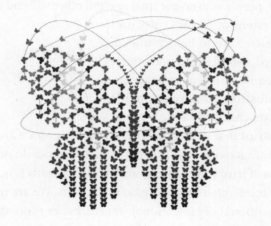

Collapse of Trust
Distrusting the establishment

Trust matters. Trust in traditional organizations and institutions is collapsing, but trust in ourselves and in our peers is growing.

"If people who have to work together in an enterprise trust one another because they are all operating according to a common set of ethical norms, doing business costs less," Francis Fukuyama writes in his book, Trust. "Such a society will be better able to innovate organizationally, since the high degree of trust will permit a wide variety of social relationships to emerge.

"By contrast, people who do not trust one and other will end up cooperating only under a system of formal rules and regulations, which have to be negotiated, agreed to, litigated, and enforced, sometimes by coercive means. This legal apparatus, serving as a substitute for trust, entails what economists call 'transaction costs.'

Distrust is tax in the digital economy.

Widespread distrust in a society, in other words, imposes a kind of tax on all forms of economic activity, a tax that high-trust societies do not have to pay."

The collapse of trust in organizations and figureheads is not a new trend, but it has been accelerated by the digital revolution. We are now reaching a point where traditional organizational structures are more distrusted than trusted and the implications for the future of our societies and economies are substantial. The classical organizational structure for humans for thousands of years has involved a leader / king / ceo / god who is revered and unquestioned. Around the king is a bureaucracy / establishment and outside all this are the citizens / customers / faithful. There is a clear hierarchy, a clear power structure. This model is failing. It will be replaced by a much flatter, collaborative, "collective intelligence" model.

In the old model, laws and orders came from above. Communication was one-way. Information was strictly controlled. Secrecy and mystery were promoted. Leaders were mythologized. They had "supernatural" powers. They were special, chosen. They were not like us. It was important that the employee / customer not really know how things actually worked. They were made to believe in the all-powerful god / brand / institution and in the almost magical powers of the great leader. It was classical blind trust.

For this sort of organizational culture to thrive you need three conditions to be in place:

1. A general population that has limited education and access to information.
2. The tools of organization and information sources to be tightly controlled by those in power.
3. A promise to the general population that their basic needs are being met, and that they can look forward to the future. That they are not alone. That they are part of the organizational tribe and family. That while they must know their place, they indeed have a place.

In the digital world, people have never been better educated and never more insecure. With the Web, they have never had better access to information. The Internet is the greatest organizational structure ever invented. It is overflowing with cheap—often free—tools that allow anyone to organize.

Now, the Millennial generation are here and they are very skeptical and demanding. (Those born from the early 1980s to early 2000s.) They are better educated but poorer than their parents.

Poorer and better educated means more questioning, skeptical.

Millennial is an attitude. The middle class is shrinking, becoming poorer and more cynical. Distrust in the establishment is growing across all generations.

- Confidence in societal institutions went up and down over time but hit its lowest point in the early 2000's. (Gallup, 2010)
- In 1958, more than 70% of US citizens said they trusted government always or most of the time. By 2010, that had dropped to just over 20%. (Pew)
- In 1975, 68% of US citizens said that they had a great deal or quite a lot of confidence in organized religion. By 2011, that had dropped to 44%. (Gallup)
- 77% of UK citizens said that they believed in God in 1968. By 2004, it was 44%. (News Batch)
- In 1997, 53% of US citizens said they had a great deal or a fair amount of trust in the media. By 2013, it had dropped to 40%, its lowest level on record. (Gallup)

- Between 2010 and 2015, US financial-services firms got the lowest possible score from consumers. (Reputation Institute)

Why we trust brands less: the BP story

In modern societies, the only group that is still heavily brand loyal are children. "My 9-year-old son just had to have Converse hi-tops," Geoffrey James wrote for INC in 2014. "However, that kind of brand loyalty is an artifact of immaturity. Children and child-like minds are easily impressed by celebrity endorsements. In any case, there's no loyalty there; next year I have no doubt my son will want some other brand just as avidly. As he matures, my son will probably (hopefully) reach the conclusion shared by the majority of educated adults: that brand is meaningless as a predictor of quality because, aside from the logo, it's all the same junk made in the same factories."

According to McKinsey, traditional TV advertising was one-third as effective in 2010 as it was 1990. In 1986, almost 80% of US car buyers bought the same car as their household had historically owned, according CNW Research. By 2009, that figure had dropped to just over 20%.

"Your customers have fewer reasons to be loyal than ever before and are really less loyal than they've ever been before," said Emily Collins, analyst at Forrester Research in 2014. "This is because empowered customers are now in control. They want control over the interactions they have with brands."

The 2010 BP oil spill in the Gulf of Mexico "is considered the largest accidental marine oil spill in the history of the petroleum industry," according to Wikipedia. It was not what the branding experts envisioned when ten years previously when they rebranded BP as a "Beyond Petroleum" company.

"BP has unveiled a new 'green' brand image, in an attempt to win over environmentally aware consumers," the BBC reported in 2000. "The new green, white and yellow logo replaces the BP shield and is designed to show the company's commitment to the environment and solar power." The BP branding approach was described as "a prescient model of credible corporate social responsibility," and won lots of advertising awards.

> In the old model, you turned lies into truth with clever marketing.

The green BP branding approach worked very well initially. Customers believed the persuasive advertising and began to rate BP as a new age, environmentally friendly green company. A 2007 Landor survey found that BP performed better than any of its peers. In 2007, BP won a gold Effie from the American Marketing Association. Its campaign was described as "a landmark platform for a company trying to change the way the world uses, and thinks about, the fuels that are vital to human progress."

The problem was that none of this was true. While in the 1980s and 1990s, BP had indeed invested heavily in alternative energy, by the time it was launching its new "Beyond Petroleum" branding campaign, it was aggressively divesting in such technologies and focusing almost exclusively on oil. It shut down its solar division, scrapped its alternative energy business, and put all its wind farms up for sale.

During this "Beyond Petroleum" period, BP was racking up one of the worst safety records possible. "BP has been fined by US Occupational Safety and Health Administration 760 times," Business Insider wrote in 2010. "By contrast, oil giant ExxonMobil has been fined only once." The article goes on to state that:

- In 2007, a BP pipeline spilled 200,000 gallons of crude into the Alaskan wilderness.
- The US Justice Department required the company to pay approximately $353 million as part of an agreement to defer prosecution on charges that the company conspired to manipulate the propane gas market.
- In two separate disasters prior to Deepwater Horizon, 30 BP workers were killed and more than 200 were seriously injured.
- According to the Center for Public Integrity, between 2007 and 2010, BP refineries in Ohio and Texas accounted for 97% of the "egregious, willful" violations handed out by authorities.

"To many, the 'Beyond Petroleum' campaign has always been ludicrous," PR Watch stated in 2010. "Despite, or maybe because of its history of fatal accidents, environmental disasters, fines and public deceit, BP is still trying to greenwash its image. Its Web pages are filled with bogus statements, like 'We try to work in ways that will benefit the communities and habitats where we do business—and earn the world's respect.'"

BP knew that it could use marketing, PR and advertising to tell the world that black was green. And for years it got away with it. However, in the digital world it is much more difficult to get away with spin and deception. The old model is broken. The new model requires transparency and an honest conversation with the customer.

Financial industry puts customers last

Financial institutions in the US are totally opposed to having to adhere to a "fiduciary standard," according to Jon Picoult of Watermark Consulting. A fiduciary standard basically expects that you should put the interests of your customers first. Financial institutions are flabbergasted that they should be expected to do such a ridiculous thing.

> The financial industry business model is to exploit its loyal customers.

For years, financial institutions have depended on customer ignorance, apathy and loyalty in order to maximize their profits. Customers are waking up. A 2015 worldwide survey of banking customers by Capgemini and Efma found major increases in the number of customers who intend to leave their banks. Globally, more than 50% of Millennials intend to change banks.

In 2014, an Ernst & Young global survey found that customers have very low trust in insurance companies. "Further, the survey results reveal that far more insurance consumers actually switch insurers than express an intention to switch—an almost unprecedented finding in market research," the survey stated. 67% of insurance customers would consider purchasing

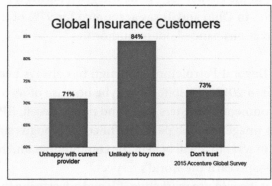

Customer attitudes towards insurance companies

insurance products from organizations other than insurers, according to a survey published by Accenture in 2014.

Ripping off loyal customers was the old model of doing business for the insurance industry. "The curious, but obviously profitable business model, in which new customers get wooed with discounts and special deals, while the oldest, most loyal, best customers are 'thanked' with bills that escalate over time," is how TIME described it in 2012.

According to Anna Tims, writing in the UK Guardian in 2014, "Insurance companies are notorious for penalising loyal customers." In a modern, educated, search-driven, social media society, this classic old model approach results in disloyalty, distrust, switching and churn. "Companies are adept at chasing new customers while watching the churn," Keith Pearce, Vice President, Solutions Marketing at Genesys states. "Why else would they spend around $500B on advertising and acquiring new customers, $50B on CRM spend, and just $9B on the call centre (Ovum)?" If you don't regularly shop around for your home and auto insurance, you're going to get ripped off by your current insurer, the Consumer Federation of America warned in 2014.

> Today, practically nobody trusts the media.

Media in the pocket of special interests
93% of 18-29 year olds in the USA think the media is biased, according to a

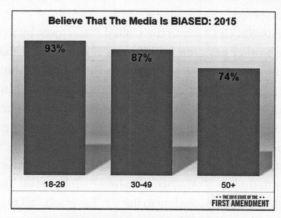

Believe That The Media Is BIASED: 2015

93% — 18-29
87% — 30-49
74% — 50+

•• THE 2015 STATE OF THE ••
FIRST AMENDMENT

2015 study of attitudes towards media bias

2015 USA State of the First Amendment survey.

So, why have people lost trust in the media? Let me give you a small example from Ireland. During the 2000s, Ireland had an irrational housing bubble and then a ruinous bust.

"It is not too difficult to identify a housing bubble in the making, based on simple indicators such as the P/E (price/earnings) ratio and the price-to-income ratio," University College Dublin academic, Dr Julien Mercille, wrote in his report on the Irish housing bubble. "This is what a few analysts did, such as The Economist magazine, which stated in 2002 that Ireland's real estate market had been 'displaying bubble-like' symptoms". However, the Irish media were almost without exception cheerleaders for the booming property market."

> Vastly overinflated CEO pay bears no relation to value.

Why might that be? Could it be that the Irish Times, the Irish newspaper of "record," owned MyHome.ie, a major property website? Or that Independent News & Media, the largest newspaper group in Ireland, owned PropertyNews.com? Could it possibly be that the Irish media gorged on property advertising as its journalists sang: "Buy! Buy! Buy!"?

The 1% trust deficit

There is a growing disconnect and distrust between the top 1% of society and everyone else. If this breach of trust keeps growing, it will not end well for any party involved.

During the 1990s, CEO pay in the United States grew by 535%. (Business Week) Average worker pay grew by 32%, just slightly higher than inflation at 27%. (Bureau of Labor Statistics, Consumer Price Index) The stock market grew at an average of 297% and corporate profits grew by 116%. (Standard & Poor, Bureau of Economic Analysis). Something doesn't compute. CEO pay grew by 535% while profits grew by 116%, while worker pay stagnated.

If you think that's bad, it got worse in the new decade. Incomes actually fell for the bottom 90%. In fact, it was the top 1% who saw the vast majority of income growth during 2000-2010. (Pavlina R. Tcherneva, Thomas Piketty, Emmanuel Saez, N.B.E.R.) According to the UK Telegraph, "CEOs of Standard & Poor 500 companies made 354 times the average wages of US workers in 2012."

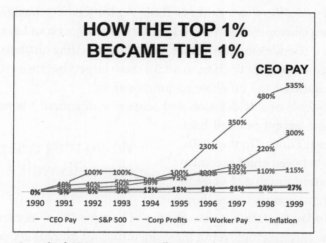

**HOW THE TOP 1%
BECAME THE 1%**

CEO PAY

Growth of CEO pay versus ordinary worker pay: 1990-1999

Even if you believe the fairytale that superhero CEOs create all the profits, they still have for years been getting pay rises that are four times greater than the value they have "supernaturally" been creating. Are CEOs really 354 times more valuable and brilliant than average workers? Well, no. "It's safe to say that CEOs are, overall, a talented bunch, but that's not what separates them from other professionals, nor is it the main reason their firms succeed or fail," Walter Frick wrote for Harvard Business Review in 2015. "Certainly it doesn't come close to explaining why they're so well paid. Put another way, CEOs matter, just less than many people think. Instead, luck, and yes, bias, play a far larger role in determining who ends up leading companies, and whether they are fired or end up industry leaders."

Then how have CEOs and other senior managers ended up getting these stratospheric sums of money every year? Because they can. Because they've spun a really good story. There is absolutely no logical, scientific, business or other reason. It's runaway greed, a tsunami of grand delusion. The boards who allocate these salaries and bonuses belong to a virtuous circle of other CEOs and senior executives. They are a Big Boy Santa Claus Club: "Who votes for more presents this year!? We do! We do! Bigger and better!!"

"Simply put, those at the top feel entitled to the lion's share of the money 'their' companies earn, and managerial egos are threatened when subordinates speak their minds in the workplace and when they don't just do what managers tell them to do." So states James O'Toole, senior fellow in business ethics at Santa Clara University. The Volkswagen diesel emissions scandal, for example, looks like a classic example of senior management setting unattainable targets that forced employees to cheat to attain these targets because everyone was afraid to question the infallible senior managers.

The bubble of elite delusion and sense of entitlement has never as bad as it is now, except perhaps back in Medieval Times. "In the 1950s, the ratio between chief executive remuneration and that of a typical worker in the company was about

When trust disappears, fear sells well.

20 to 1. Today, the ratio between the pay of Fortune 500 chief executives and that of the average employee in these organizations exceeds 200 to 1," Nancy Koehn wrote for The Washington Post in 2014.

At the same time, the vast majority of workers and families are seeing their financial world contract. Their incomes are barely rising. It's becoming harder and harder just to get by. That's not fair, of course, but fairness is not the issue. It's not sustainable either. Trust is collapsing and society will grind to a halt as more and more people get disillusioned and disengage. Why do you think so many people are voting for anti-establishment candidates in elections?

"Workers around the globe have been finding it harder to juggle the demands of work and the rest of life in the past five years," Brigid Schulte, wrote for the Washington Post in 2015, quoting a report from Ernst & Young. "Many are working longer hours, deciding to delay or forgo having children, discontinuing education, or struggling to pay tuition for their children. Professional workers in companies that shed employees in the Great Recession are still doing the work of two or more people and working longer hours. Salaries have stagnated, and costs continue to rise."

The result? A trust deficit that is becoming a chasm. According to the Edelman Trust Barometer, in 2015 just 31% of people in developed countries trusted CEOs, whereas 61% of people in developing countries trusted them. No surprise that the better educated and more informed people are the less they trust such figureheads. Much of the old model of management has been based on the ignorance and acquiescence of employees, customers and societies in general, and the use of marketing and advertising to spin the "story."

"If our civilization is to survive, we must break with the habit of deference to great men," philosopher Karl Popper wrote in 1945, though he could have been writing it in 2015. The Great Man Syndrome (and they are invariably men) is a disease whereby a very intelligent, hardworking, visionary man—once he gets promoted to senior management—begins to think he is superhuman and God-like, all-powerful, all-seeing, and thus requires a gargantuan remuneration package and unquestioned loyalty. Without great men, the Great Man Syndrome posits, society would collapse, value would be destroyed and life wouldn't be worth living.

There is no question that great men have a contribution to make. But their contributions are nearly always exaggerated and mythologized, because we love stories about individuals, not about groups or committees or networks. Humans live in groups but mythologize individuals. Groups are just not sexy or heroic or inspiring. The media and Hollywood feed our desire for superstars. We want them to be exotic, to be superrich, to be so above us that we can look up and up to them. Until now, that is. Society is changing. The age of the Great Man is approaching its twilight and the age of collaboration, of the team, of the group, is emerging.

The importance of Great Men are vastly overhyped.

The Great Man myth is a fabrication, a lie. Sure, there are always exceptions, but the cold, hard, immutable facts shine a harsh and unforgiving light on our superhero executives:

- "The more CEOs are paid, the worse the firm does over the next three years, as far as stock performance and even accounting performance," Michael Cooper, co-author of a study at the University of Utah's David Eccles School of Business, states. The worst performance was found in the 150 firms with the highest-paid CEOs. High-pay CEOs, with high overconfidence and high tenure, return 22% worse in shareholder value over three years as compared to their peers.
- For large, established companies, "it's very hard to show that picking one well-qualified CEO over another has a major impact on corporate performance," Michael Dorff, author of the book, Indispensable and Other Myths, writes.

- If the company with the two-hundred-and-fiftieth-most-talented CEO suddenly managed to hire the most talented CEO its value would increase by a mere 0.016 per cent, a study by Xavier Gabaix and Augustin Landier found.
- Higher pay fails to promote better performance, a study by Philippe Jacquart and J. Scott Armstrong found.
- Variations in company performance account for only about 5 percent of the variation between how much companies pay their top executives, a Journal of Management study found.

"There is a connection between the biggest CEO checks and companies that have been making deals, such as going public, doing big mergers or divestitures and reorganizations," Tim Mullaney wrote. "A KPMG study indicates that 83% of merger deals did not boost shareholder returns," George Bradt wrote for Forbes in 2015. According to Peter Clark, writing for Quartz in 2013, more than 20 articles and papers show "that two-thirds or more of all deals 'fail.'" So why do mergers happen? Because of the ego and greed of great men and their desire for a supernatural bonus for doing such great deals.

Decline of experts

As Big Data rolls out and the evidence of what actually happened and is happening comes in, one thing is becoming starkly clear. The "experts"—who contain many of the Great Men, who we are getting these supernatural remunerations and those "advising" them—are being proved wrong time and time again. That is not surprising. In an ever increasingly complex world, only a fool would predict the future and only an idiot would listen to them. Big Data is shining a harsh beam of cold light on the expertise of Great Men.

Make the customer the expert, not yourself.

"Increasingly, expertise is losing the respect that for years had earned it premiums in any market where uncertainty was present and complex knowledge valued", Bill Fischer wrote for Harvard Business Review in 2015. "Along with it, we are shedding our reverence for 'expert evaluation,' losing our regard for our Michelin guides and casting our lot in with the peer-generated Yelps of the world."

What's the implication for you? Stop trying to become the expert. Facilitate the customer to become expert, to do things, to learn, to control as much as possible. Create designs that make them the expert. Give them the digital tools and controls that make them the expert, and then learn from them in order to make these tools more powerful, simpler, faster.

"Have you ever thought economists were far more confident in their statements about the world than they had any right to be? Well, now there's proof." So writes Justin Fox in an article for the Harvard Business Review. Fox was writing about a study by Emre Soyer and Robin Hogarth who had asked 257 economists a range of questions about probabilities of various outcomes and found that, "The economists did a really bad job of answering the questions. They paid too much attention to the averages, and too little to the uncertainties inherent in them, thereby displaying too much confidence."

In the new model, you must learn to love uncertainty. You must accept that very often you will not know the answer, and that's okay once you know how to find out the answer. You must learn to be highly skeptical and always looking for evidence.

Rating agencies such as Moody's, S&P, and Fitch Ratings were the cheerleaders of the sub-prime mortgage orgy, which was a key cause of the 2007 financial crisis and global recession. These agencies have huge power in the world. Many governments and investment institutions follow their advice in an almost unquestioning manner. These oracle-like rating agencies gave their highest ratings to "over three trillion dollars of loans to homebuyers with bad credit and undocumented incomes," according to Wikipedia. In other words, these rating agencies gave their highest ratings to the worst possible type of loans that any self-respecting loan shark would avoid. Now, why would they do that?

After the financial crash, these agencies switched from irrational exuberance to deathly pessimism. In June 2012, for example, Moody's predicted that Irish house prices were set to decline by a further 20%. As you can see from the following chart by the Irish Central Statistics Office, things didn't quite work out that way. Prices hit their bottom in 2012 and have risen steady since then. So, these rating agencies are pretty clueless and yet they get paid huge quantities of money for their terrible advice.

"To a certain extent, investors have ignored Moody's and other ratings

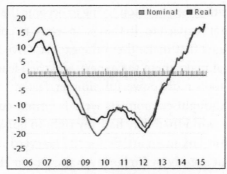

Irish house price growth: 2006-2013

agencies," Bloomberg stated in 2015. "In almost half the instances, yields on government bonds fall when a rating action by S&P and Moody's suggests they should climb, according to data compiled by Bloomberg on 314 upgrades, downgrades and outlook changes going back as far as the 1970s."

Big Data and the Internet are lifting the carpet and there's a mountain of dirt underneath it. Big Data is shining a floodlight. Social media is asking the questions. Digital's natural color is transparent. It's hard to hide in a digital world.

> Simplicity equals trust. Trust in use. Complexity equals distrust.

Complexity creates distrust

Old model organizations thrive on complexity. It was part of the advantage they had over their customers. Thirty years ago, a typical customer looked at something complex and said: "I must be stupid." Today, people look at complexity coming from organizations and say: "They must be stupid." The customer has transformed. The organization has not. Today, complexity feeds distrust. We trust in use. Simplicity feeds trust.

This change is not good for a whole range of industries whose basic business model is to confuse and distract the customer. Scott Adams, creator of Dilbert, called these companies "confusopolies" in his 1997 book Dilbert Future. "The word is a portmanteau of confusion and monopoly (or rather oligopoly), defining it as 'a group of companies with similar products who intentionally confuse customers instead of competing on price'," Wikipedia states. "Examples of industries in which confusopolies exist (according to

Adams) include telephone service, insurance, mortgage loans, banking, and financial services."

Every time you do something that makes things simpler and easier for your customers, you build trust. Thus, your job is critical to customer trust building. However, you walk a tightrope because complexity and customer-exploitation practices that may be woven into your organization's business model and culture. There will be a lot of powerful interests keen to keep the status quo. You deal with this by flooding your organization with the poor experience customers are getting. You must show, again and again, the core causes of disloyalty and switching.

In the old model, life was made easiest for the most powerful, and it was made deliberately complex for the least powerful. You can hide lots of things behind complexity. You can rip people off with complex pricing. You can strip them of their rights with complex language. You can exclude them with complex knowledge. You can force loyalty on them by making it very complex to switch brands. In the mystery lies the margin, as they say. (Or, as some have said, "in the margin lies the mystery." Or as Jeff Bezos said: "In the margin lies my opportunity.") In the complexity lay much of the profit that fed the bonuses in the old model world. But this complexity is exactly what new competitors will attack.

There is a direct link between corruption and complexity.

The Mystery of Capital by Hernando De Soto is one of the most impressive books I have ever read. In it, De Soto develops a theory of why some countries succeed while others fail. He found that there is a direct link between corruption and complexity. Governments and other organizations within corrupt societies force you to go through a whole host of unnecessary and complex steps if you want to do anything with them. They use these unnecessary steps as a toll booth to either charge you an unnecessary fee or bribe.

Dimitris is a small business owner in Greece. According to a TIME article, he estimates he has paid "about a fifth of his revenue in bribes—to tax collectors, health inspectors, police and other officials". Small firms "are essentially obligated to conduct business this way," he says. "There are so many legal barriers to conducting business that they'll shut you down otherwise." This is a core reason why Greece has been in such a crisis: a crisis of complexity, a crisis of trust.

UK citizens distrust the European Union more than any other member country. According to a YouGov survey the number one reason for this distrust it not—as might be expected—loss of national power, but rather too much EU bureaucracy. Bureaucracy is just another word for complexity.

From an old model perspective, there are compelling reasons to promote complexity. For starters, complexity "protects" the jobs of those who have designed the complex systems. Their expertise and experience is essential to its running. Complexity is a lock-in for customers. The more complex an organization's systems, products and services are, and the more they can intertwine and embed them into the customer's world, the higher the switching costs become: complexity creates addiction, dependency. But as digital simplifies the landscape and as services move to the Cloud, the switching costs drop precipitously and before you know it there's a stampede of customers to the exits.

I never knew I was so popular. When I went through the process of switching my pension, everyone wanted to meet me. When I asked about basic prices (that should have been on the websites), I was told that I would be given those prices in the meeting. They just wanted to meet little old me, but little old me didn't want to meet them. Because I have been through these "face-to-face" shakedown meetings once too often. They think that if they give you tea and biscuits and look you in the eye, you'll fall under the magic of their sales spin, and they'll be able to charge you a higher rate. That firm handshake and that cup of tea will cost you a lot.

The old model of complexity is dying on its feet. "Business-to-business (B2B) buyers now favor do-it-yourself online options for researching and buying products and services, and they are demanding that B2B sellers fully enable

Trust is shifting towards friends and "people like me."

those digital paths to purchase," Andy Hoar from Forrester Research has stated. "Yet too many of today's B2B companies still insist that B2B buyers interact with sales reps in order to complete a purchase." However, Forrester estimates that by 2020 there will be a million less B2B salespeople in the U.S.

as more and more customers demand digital self-service.

People trust their friends

While there is a collapse in trust in institutions and in Great Men, people are much more likely to trust their friends and family and people like them. (Although the evidence is showing that they are becoming less likely to trust strangers.) According to the Edelman Trust Barometer, in 2015 people trusted people like themselves twice as much as they trusted CEOs.

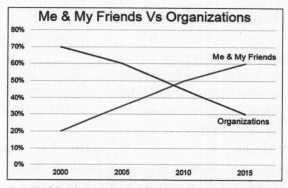

Trust in friends versus trust in organizations: 2000-2015

In 2000, around 70% of people still put their trust in brands and organizations, with only about 20% looking to their peers. By 2015, it had pretty much reversed. Social media is me and my friends, not me and my brands. It's the customer economy, it's the peer economy.

Customers today trust action. They trust what they can do quickly and easily. Trust is based on use. Mistrust is immediate when the thing to be used is hidden behind such fake language as: "It's now even easier to use; We're delighted to announce the launch of this fantastic new feature; Because we care about our customers so much ..." Customers couldn't care less about what you have to say. They want to see results. They'll try to use it and then they'll judge. Blind, long-term trust is a thing of the past. It's dead and won't come back. You earn or lose trust every time a customer uses your product or service. Customers trust those who give them control—who put them in control—of their lives. They distrust those who try to control them.

Digital design is about putting the customer in control, as Timothy Morey,

Theo Forbath and Allison Schoop wrote for Harvard Business Review in 2015. They gave an example of a cardiac monitoring system where, "Participating cardiac patients wear an e-monitor, which collects ECG data and transmits it via smartphone to medical professionals and other caregivers. The patients see all their own data and control how much data goes to whom, using a browser and an app. They can set up networks of health care providers, of family and friends, or of fellow users and patients, and send each different information. This patient-directed approach is a radical departure from the tradition of paternalistic medicine that carries over to many medical devices even today, with which the patient doesn't own his data or even have access to it."

Better informed patients are easier to treat and get well quicker.

"Why should we care about the fact that patients, families and primary health care providers want information about what happens before, during and after treatment?" Eirik Hafver Rønjum of the Norwegian Department of Health asks. "Altruism? Yes, maybe. But I think the key to gaining acceptance for focusing on patient needs, is building a business case around those needs. In our case we can point to the studies showing that well-informed patients are less costly to treat than patients without this knowledge. Voila! We now have the business case, and the Web is no longer a nice-to-have add on to the core activity at the hospitals, it has become part of the core business, namely a part of the treatment."

The better informed customer is a better customer. Build up the evidence that shows this. Target a senior executive who you believe can be won over and feed them with customer experience data. Show them videos of customers failing. And show them how, when the customer succeeds, the organization succeeds. Because in this new model of transparency, doing right by the customer is not just the right thing to do—it's the clever thing to do.

References

Fukuyama, F. *Trust: The Social Virtues and the Creation of Prosperity,* Free Press, 1995

James, G. *Brand Loyalty Is (Almost) Dead,* Feb. 2014
http://www.inc.com/geoffrey-james/brand-loyalty-is-almost-dead.html

Wikipedia. *Oil spill*
https://en.wikipedia.org/wiki/Oil_spill

BBC News. *BP Goes Green,* July 2000
http://news.bbc.co.uk/2/hi/business/849475.stm

Accenture. *Insurance Customers Would Consider Buying Insurance from Internet Giants, According to Accenture's Global Research,* Feb. 2014
https://newsroom.accenture.com/subjects/research-surveys/insurance-customers-would-consider-buying-insurance-from-internet-giants-according-to-accentures-global-research.htm

Veneziani, V. *BP's Horrible Safety Record: It's Got 760 OSHA Fines, Exxon Has Just 1,* Business Insider, June 2010
http://www.businessinsider.com/bp-has-been-fined-by-osha-760-times-has-an-awful-track-record-for-safety-2010-6?IR=T

Landman, A. *BP's "Beyond Petroleum" Campaign Losing its Sheen,* May 2010
http://www.prwatch.org/news/2010/05/9038/bps-beyond-petroleum-campaign-losing-its-sheen

Tuttle, B. *Proof That Loyalty is For Suckers: Best Customers Get Penalized With Higher Bills,* Sept. 2012
http://business.time.com/2012/09/06/proof-that-loyalty-is-for-suckers-best-customers-get-penalized-with-higher-bills/

Tims, A. *When it Comes to Insurance, Loyalty Only Pays the Provider,* The Guardian, Nov. 2014
http://www.theguardian.com/money/2014/nov/06/tesco-insurance-loyalty-quotes-price-new-customers

Pearce, K. *Reducing Customer Effort – The Hidden Key to Reducing Customer Churn in the Retail Industry,* Mar. 2013
http://theforum.social/customerquality/Resources/ArticleId/1883

Consumer Federation of America, *Reimagining Customer Relationships: Key Findings from the EY Global Consumer Insurance Survey 2014*
https://static.rasset.ie/documents/news/ey-global-customer-insurance-survey.pdf

State of the First Amendment Surveys, 2015 *State of the First Amendment Survey,* 2015
www.newseuminstitute.org/first-amendment-center/state-of-the-first-amendment/

Mercille, J. *The Role of the Media in Propping up Ireland's Housing Bubble*, Apr. 2013
https://www.socialeurope.eu/2013/04/the-role-of-the-media-in-propping-up-irelands-housing-bubble/

Liberto, J. CEOs *Earn 354 Times More than Average Worker*, Apr. 2013
http://money.cnn.com/2013/04/15/news/economy/ceo-pay-worker/

Frick, W. *Are Successful CEOs Just Lucky?* Harvard Business Review, Nov. 2015
https://hbr.org/2015/11/are-successful-ceos-just-lucky

O'Toole, J. *U.S. Employees Are Disengaged—and Mismanaged*, Strategy Business, July 2013
http://www.strategy-business.com/article/US-Employees-Are-Disengaged-and-Mismanaged?gko=e1ff3

Koehn, *Nancy F. Great Men, Great Pay? Why CEO Compensation is Sky High*, June 2014
https://www.washingtonpost.com/opinions/great-men-great-pay-why-ceo-compensation-is-sky-high/2014/06/12/6e49d796-d227-11e3-9e25-188ebe1fa93b_story.html

Schulte, B. Millennials *Want a Work-Life Balance. Their Bosses Just Don't Get Why*, The Washington Post, May 2015
https://www.washingtonpost.com/local/millennials-want-a-work-life-balance-their-bosses-just-dont-get-why/2015/05/05/1859369e-f376-11e4-84a6-6d7c67c50db0_story.html

Popper, K. *The Open Society and Its Enemies*, Princeton University Press, USA, 2013

Adams, S. *The Highest-Paid CEOs Are the Worst Performers, New Study Says*, Forbes, June 2014
http://www.forbes.com/sites/susanadams/2014/06/16/the-highest-paid-ceos-are-the-worst-performers-new-study-says/#33e18a4e293a

Dorff, M. *Indispensable and Other Myths: Why the CEO Pay Experiment Failed and How to Fix It*, University of California Press, USA, 2014

Gabaix, X. & Landier, A. *Why Has CEO Pay Increased So Much?* Apr. 2007
http://economics.mit.edu/files/1769

Jacquart, P. & Armstrong, J. S. *Are Top Executives Paid Enough? An Evidence Based Review*, 2013
https://pdfs.semanticscholar.org/7ba7/24cfd059bd0a6f18fa7c21c6935419eabeb6.pdf

Mullaney, T. *Why Corporate CEO Pay is So high, and Going Higher?*, CNBC, May 2015
http://www.cnbc.com/2015/05/18/why-corporate-ceo-pay-is-so-high-and-going-higher.html

Bradt, G. *83% of Mergers Fail -- Leverage a 100-Day Action Plan for Success Instead*, Forbes, Jan. 2015
http://www.forbes.com/sites/georgebradt/2015/01/27/83-mergers-fail-leverage-a-100-day-value-acceleration-plan-for-success-instead/#3bd8f796b349

Mark, P. *Why We Keep Coming Back for Mergers Even Though They Don't Work,* June 2013
http://qz.com/97250/why-we-keep-coming-back-for-mergers-even-though-they-dont-work/

Fischer, B. *The End of Expertise,* Harvard Business Review, Oct. 2015
https://hbr.org/2015/10/the-end-of-expertise

Justin F. *Economists Are Overconfident. So Are You,* Harvard Business Review, June 2012
https://hbr.org/2012/06/economists-are-overconfident-s/

RTE News. *Moody's sees another 20% fall in house prices,* June 2012
http://www.rte.ie/news/business/2012/0615/325104-moodys-sees-another-20-fall-in-house-prices/

Global Property Guide: *House Prices Worldwide*
http://www.globalpropertyguide.com/real-estate-house-prices/I#ireland

Meakin, L. *Euro Yields Drift Further from Ratings After $531 Billion of QE,* Bloomberg Business, Dec. 2015
http://www.bloomberg.com/news/articles/2015-12-22/euro-yields-drift-further-from-ratings-after-531-billion-of-qe

Wikipedia. Confusopoly
https://en.wikipedia.org/wiki/Confusopoly

Adams, S. *The Dilbert Future: Thriving on Stupidity in the 21st Century,* Boxtree, Sept. 1998
https://www.goodreads.com/book/show/53888.The_Dilbert_Future

Itano, N. *Taxing Times in Greece,* Time, Feb. 2010
http://content.time.com/time/magazine/article/0,9171,1958721,00.html

Soto, de H. T*he Mystery of Capital: Why Capitalism Triumphs in the West and Fails Everywhere Else,* Bantam Press/Random House, 2000

Hoar, A. *It's Here...The Forrester Wave: B2B Commerce Suites,* Q2 2015, June 2015
http://blogs.forrester.com/andy_hoar

Edelman. 2015 *Edelman Trust Barometer: Executive Summary, 2015*
http://www.edelman.com/insights/intellectual-property/2015-edelman-trust-barometer/trust-and-innovation-edelman-trust-barometer/executive-summary/

McGovern, G. *Comments on What Really Matters: Focusing on Top Tasks, Eirik Hafver Rønjum comments,* A List Apart, Apr. 2015
http://alistapart.com/comments/what-really-matters-focusing-on-top-tasks

Morey et al. *Customer Data: Designing for Transparency and Trust,* Harvard Business Review, May 2015
https://hbr.org/2015/05/customer-data-designing-for-transparency-and-trust

Picoult, J. *Reforming a Tone-Deaf Industry,* Barron's, Mar. 2015
http://www.watermarkconsult.net/docs/Reforming-A-Tone-Deaf-Industry-(Barrons).pdf

7
MARKETING: FROM GETTING TO GIVING ATTENTION

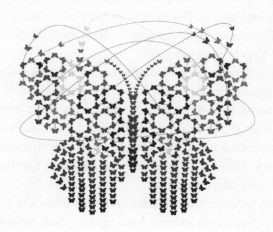

Marketing: From Getting to Giving Attention
Pavlov's Dogs are disobeying

You are as likely to get hit by lightning as you are to click on an online banner ad. And even if you do click on that ad, the chances that you'll buy something based on the ad are virtually nonexistent, according to a study by Pretarget and ComScore. "88 percent of business buyers believe that online content has played a major to moderate role in vendor selection," according to a 2014 Chief Marketing Officer survey. "The bad news: Only 9% of buyers trust vendor websites."

The golden heyday of marketing and advertising is on the wane. The magic is wearing thin. The clever and creative pitches have been used once too often. People aren't watching as much anymore. People aren't listening. Some organizations may still be increasing their advertising spend but that's because the effectiveness of advertising is declining and therefore you need to spend more to get the same effect.

Traditional marketing has a long history of practicing the "dark arts" of emotional manipulation. Some of the most basic emotional triggers are to do with association. Find out the thing that people really love and associate your product with it. If you do it right, then they'll love your product by association. These mass marketing techniques have been used extensively for almost 100 years. They are dependent on a relatively uneducated, gullible, vain or emotionally-insecure public.

Ivan Petrovich Pavlov was a Russian scientist who rang a bell every time he fed his dogs. On seeing the food, his dogs salivated. After a while, Pavlov just rang the bell and didn't provide any food. The dogs still salivated because they now associated the ringing of the bell with food even when there was no food present. When marketers and advertisers discovered Pavlov's research, they salivated. Find those—often subconscious—emotional triggers and ring that bell. The bell has been ringing ever since. However, in today's media saturated, attention deficit world, customers are becoming more and more deaf and blind to these increasingly out-of-date techniques.

How does the traditional advertising industry respond? By ringing the bell louder. And by coming up with ever more clever techniques like "native advertising," a type of advertising that pretends to be editorial copy. Before Volkswagen was almost suffocated by the diesel fumes scandal, it was happily pushing native advertising in magazines such as Wired, claiming "how diesel was re-engineered," and how it had become "cleaner and more future forward."

Advertising blindness

Traditional advertising and marketing are in denial and this is a challenge for you because it is often advertising and marketing that clutters and slows down the digital environment, increasing complexity and customer annoyance. "I love a great commercial as much the next person and am in awe of the creative and strategic minds that create them," Winston Binch, Chief Digital Officer at Deutsch LA states. Now, only a delusional advertising mad man could possibly make a statement like that. Binch does realize that the times are changing, though. He suggests that "agencies need to make a greater case with clients for authenticity." Agreed. But then he goes on to give an example of this "authenticity". "Last year, our Super Bowl teaser for Volkswagen, 'The Barkside,' featured a bunch of dogs barking the theme to Star Wars. It didn't include any product and received 14 million views in two weeks." Authenticity?

> For traditional advertisers, authenticity equals barking dogs.

Do these much vaunted Super Bowl ads actually work? "Meaning: do they generate sales or other value for the brands and companies that pay so much to have them produced and aired?" Marketingland asked in 2015. "The assumption is yes. But the empirical evidence suggests the opposite … There appears to be a profound disconnect between viewer enjoyment of the ads on game day and later buying behavior in the real world. A new survey conducted by Genesis Media found that nearly 90 percent of respondents said that they were unlikely to buy something tied to a Super Bowl ad; and roughly 75 percent of respondents said they couldn't remember ads from last year." Budweiser, which has had the second, third and fourth most watched Super Bowl ads, shipped 30 million barrels of beer in 2003, and just 16 million in 2013.

This is the dirty little secret of advertising. Great ads may have a "wow" factor but that often doesn't create much real value for the client who pays for them, which is not surprising when you understand how a traditional advertiser thinks. A senior ad executive once told me that, "The whole purpose

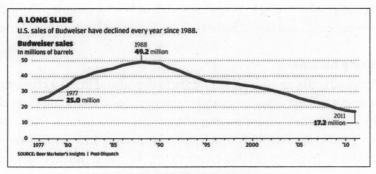

U.S. sales of Budweiser: 1977-2010

is to get our ads as talked about as possible." He didn't care about whether the ad helped sell more product. He just wanted people to talk about the ad itself. And companies pay for this stuff?

TV advertising was one-third as effective as it was in 1990, according to a study from McKinsey. "Top marketers these days are quick to point to an overarching trend in the industry," Stephanie Walden wrote for Mashable in March 2015. "With the rise of public forums such as social media, fewer companies are finding success with 'mass marketing' tactics."

Customers will do anything they can to avoid online ads.

An example of banner blindness

For years, we have been observing customers as they use websites and apps. And there is one dominant trend: if it looks anything like marketing or advertising, a great number of people will avoid and ignore it. On one website, we tested "Task A". It was a very important task for the organization, so they promoted it on the homepage. There was one huge banner dominating the page and a smaller banner in the right navigation, something like in the preceding image. Each banner had a nice smiling actor. Not one single person out of those we tested clicked on either of the banners, even though every single one of them spent a considerable amount of time on the page in question. Not one.

When we did some testing for Microsoft, we had the following task: "Does Microsoft support producing multiple copies of a Windows Embedded POSReady 2009 image, using cloning?" The answer was no. In fact, Microsoft felt that it was so important to tell the programmers that the answer was no that they made the answer a "Note" and placed it in the box in the middle of the page.

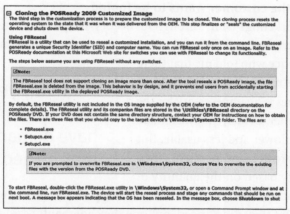

Microsoft Embedded POSReady 2009 image website page

Nearly all the programmers we tested found the right page and every single one of them who did said that the answer was yes. They were ignoring the note. It was something that was trying to get their attention, so they assumed it must contain useless information.

Advertising / marketing blindness will only grow as we have less and less attention to give and more and more things want to get that attention:

- A test of four separate page treatments by Tom Tullis, Marisa Siegel and Emily Sun found that the page with no images and no boxes got the most eye fixations.

- Another study by the same group of people for Fidelity Investments found that adding smiling faces reduced the credibility of the content in the eyes of customers.
- A study of eight versions of a particular page by GOV.UK requesting people to become organ donors found that the least effective page was the one with a group of people smiling. The most effective page had no image of people.
- A hairdressers in the UK placed a series of offers on its Facebook pages. One set of offers had professional pictures of women getting their hair done. The other had amateur pictures. The promotions with the professional pictures got 1 like and no clicks. The promotion with amateur pictures got 79 Likes and 521 clicks.

Sometimes, the customer wants to be fooled

It is not all marketing's fault. Throughout history, people have often demanded that they be tricked and fooled. I talked to a content management software salesperson once who told me that there was a features race in his industry. Most of these features were unnecessary for the typical customer. In fact, they just made the software slower and less usable. But customers were demanding them. They judged quality based on the quantity of

For many years, some customers have demanded that they be lied to.

features. What was he to do? If he wanted to keep his job, he had to keep selling them a product they didn't need, but one they adamantly said they wanted.

Ashley Madison is a site for older men who want to cheat on their wives with a younger woman. That's why on the Ashley Madison homepage there is a huge picture of a beautiful young woman. It has been estimated that about 9 out of 10 of Ashley Madison's members are men. Gizmodo reporter Annalee Newitz found out that the vast majority of these female "members" weren't even real. After analysis, it was discovered that of the estimated 5 million female members, only 12,000 of them belonged to actual, real women. "Those millions of Ashley Madison men were paying to hook up with women who appeared to have created profiles and then simply disappeared," Newitz wrote.

The facts are irrelevant to Ashley Madison men. They want to buy illusion.

Most of us, at some stage in our lives, want to buy illusion. When margarine was first invented, it was colored yellow to make it look more like butter because people would not buy a white spread. On the other hand, white bread was all the rage because it was associated with the rich. Such bread could only be made from high quality flour. But poor people demanded white bread from their bakers, so bakers started coloring the low quality flour to get more white-looking bread.

In 1858, in Bradford, in the UK, 200 people were made sick and 20 died from eating lozenges. The sweets had been coated with arsenic. "The lozenge-maker had intended to adulterate his lozenges with plaster of Paris but had bought arsenic by mistake," writes Bee Wilson in her excellent book on food adulteration called Swindled. Parents and kids were obsessed with the brightest colored sweets possible, and manufacturers obliged by coating sweets with various poisons.

Years ago, I remember having a conversation with a vegetable stall owner. He told me how it was very hard to sell organic vegetables. The organic carrots, for example, came in all shapes and sizes, but people only wanted the perfectly shaped carrots. People bought with their eyes. They still do, though less so. Organic vegetables and products are now being bought more because people are better educated and less driven by primitive emotions. The Web is the great educator and there is a global rise in awareness and consciousness. We are still driven by our emotions but we're a little bit more in control now and that can make all the difference when it comes to the role of marketing. (Unless, of course, we're an Ashley Madison marketer.)

> The future of marketing is about looking after current customers.

From getting attention to giving attention

"About 90 percent of Google's revenue is from ads, most of that on its search engine," The New York Times stated in 2015. All those billions in revenue from those tiny, innocuous 17 words of text on the search results page? This is advertising like your parents weren't used to.

The Google search engine is traditional advertising in reverse—the ads are actually useful, purposeful. That's because when it comes to search advertising, the customer is the advertiser. When you go to Google, do you see traditional graphical ads blaring out at you trying to get your attention? No, just a search box. It's waiting for you, the "advertiser." It's a blank page—a blank canvas—and you are in control. It's waiting for you to make the first move.

You place an ad in the search box: "cheap flights Dublin." The search engine notifies all those companies that sell flights that someone has placed an ad for a cheap flight to Dublin. These companies can then respond with an offer.

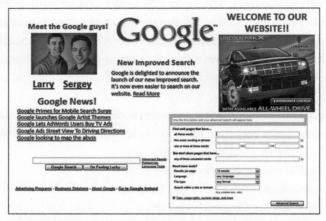

Google homepage if it was designed by traditional organization

The above is what the Google homepage might look like if it was designed by most traditional marketing-driven organizations. It would be full of clutter, organization-centricity and advertising. Would this approach succeed?

New model marketing puts the customer—particularly the current customer—in control. It's marketing that's useful. It's marketing that understands the top tasks of customers and helps them complete those tasks. It's marketing that seeks to pay attention rather than get attention. Walmart's "savings catcher" is a good example of this new approach. As Michael Schrage wrote in the Harvard Business Review in 2015, "it promises shoppers that they will never overpay for purchasing at the store. By submitting their receipt through the app, Walmart customers receive credit in their account if the product was available for a lower price elsewhere."

MeUndies makes men's and women's comfortable underwear. It doesn't reward new customers, as the vast majority of traditional marketing campaigns do. Instead, it rewards loyal customers. "We found that if users signed up at full price, they were more likely to remain loyal than users who would sign up with a discount," Dan King, head of business development, explains. "We then gave our 'full price' customers discount offers later to reward them for their loyalty, after we already had established a great relationship with them." MeUndies now attracts new customers with a higher lifetime value.

> **Make customers successful at what they have decided they want to do.**

Serve the customers' journey

A key to the new model marketing is that you go on the journey the customer has decided to go on, rather than try and convince the customer to go on your "brand" journey. Once you are helping the customer complete their journey you may make helpful suggestions to them. Make the customer successful and they become a willing listener.

Sparebanken Sogn og Fjordane in Norway used to have a very traditional banking homepage. It was full of expensive, beautifully shot pictures of make-believe customers thoroughly enjoying themselves as a direct result of being Sparebanken customers. Marketing nirvana.

Original marketing-led Sparebanken homepage

However, the page was so cluttered and full of jargon that real customers were having problems logging into their accounts. So, the bank did something radical. It removed all traditional marketing from the homepage and focused on the login process.

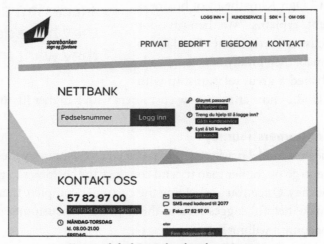

New task-led Sparebanken homepage

When I show traditional bank executives the new page, they shudder. "But we have to have the ability to market to our customers," they say. When I tell them that the new design resulted in a 500% increase in visits to the product pages, they simply won't believe their eyes or the facts.

Sparebanken Sogn og Fjordane didn't stop advertising. They just did it more cleverly. On the log out page, they placed a single, clear advertisement.

Customers had quickly and easily done what they needed to do. When they logged out, they were open to an offer, because their mind was open, because they had completed their task. This is what I call marketing at the end of the task.

Focus on what you can take away, not what you can add.

The end of the task is not the only place to communicate, of course. There are often logical progression points in tasks where appropriate communication can be very effective. This is what you have to design for. Go on the journey with the customer and make them more successful. We once worked for an

Sparebanken log out page

electronics retailer, for example, and noticed that they didn't have a clear "Buy" button at the bottom of their product pages. They had the "Buy" button at the top of the page but the product pages were often long. We got them to add the "Buy" button at the bottom of the page and sales doubled. Now, not many people got to the bottom of their product pages, but those that did tended to be very interested and ready to act. One of your greatest skills will be understanding the points in the digital journey when the person is ready to act. The Task Performance Indicator, which I will describe in detail later, is a method that helps you truly understand how customers behave in an online environment.

Make it easy

"Feeling overwhelmed, consumers want support—not increased marketing messages or 'engagement'—to more quickly and easily navigate the purchase process," Corporate Executive Board (CEB) stated in a study it published in 2012. "Brands that help consumers simplify the purchase journey have customers who are 86 percent more likely to purchase their products and 115 percent more likely to recommend their brand to others." In a study of 7,000 consumers, CEB found that 80% don't want a relationship with a brand; they just want to get something done. In a study by Havas Media in 2013, over 90% of Western consumers said they wouldn't care if most brands disappeared.

"Our research indicates that the impact of simplifying purchase decisions for consumers is four times stronger than the favored marketing strategy of engagement and is the number one driver of likelihood to buy," said Patrick Spenner, managing director at CEB.

"Customers want ease. Getting back to their busy lives quickly matters more than anything", Matthew Dixon, Nick Toman and Rick DeLisi write in the book, The Effortless Experience. "The greatest driver of disloyalty is the amount of effort you require your customers to put into their service experience. Customer effort includes repeat contacts, repeating information, channel switching (e.g. starting in Web and ending up on the phone), transfers, policies and procedures, and the general hassle factor that most service interactions create."

In 2013, The Temkin Group found that IT professionals were 55% more likely to buy from tech vendors who made life very easy for them. Only 4% said they planned buying from vendors who were very difficult to deal with.

And still the old model organizations just want to add more products, more content, more features. Why do we add new features? Dharmesh Shah, founder of HubSpot asks. Often the reply is that "It just makes sense. You're surprised that the product exists at all without this feature." Or, "A big/important customer is asking for it." Or, "It's not that hard. I think our dev team can crank it out in a weekend." Or, "A competitor just added it." Or, "It will drive revenue! Your gut is telling you that more people will buy, more people will stay, or your existing customers will spend more money if you have this feature."

> ## Complexity is the enemy of use.

While the benefits of adding new content and features can seem obvious to everyone, the costs are much less obvious. The first one is "Increase in setup time," according to Shah. More configuration, more training, more time to sell, more time for the customer to understand.

This sort of cost often remains dormant initially. You add feature/content A and nothing bad happens. Then you add B, C, D, E … At some point you reach a tipping point of complexity. Things just get harder and you can't pinpoint any one feature or piece of content as causing the problem. New features need to be promoted and this promotional content is often a huge annoyance for customers, usually getting in the way as they try and do things.

But the biggest cost of all is that if a product or service is too complex with too many features, customers simply won't use it.

This is why you need to measure use based on customer top tasks. You must figure out what is most critical to the customer and bring that up to maximum performance and then ensure it stays at maximum performance. Anything new added to the environment must prove that it is not interfering with the performance of the top tasks. You do that by constantly measuring the

Nothing kills a customer experience more than slow speeds.

top tasks. Later, I'll explain a method to clearly identify the top tasks of your customers and to measure how well they're performing.

Make it fast

Digital speeds everything up. According to Statistic Brain, the average attention span in 2015 was 8.25 seconds, down from 12 seconds in 2000. (The average attention span of a gold fish is estimated at 9 seconds.)

- For every second faster Walmart.com was able to make its pages load, it had a 2% lift in conversions.
- Firefox reduced its page load time by 2.2 seconds and had 10 million extra downloads as a result.
- Bing, Yahoo and Google found that if a search page takes more than half a second longer to load than expected, there is a significant drop in advertising revenue.

Think about it. Less than half a second impacts revenue. As a result, Google recommends webpage load times of one second or less. Larry Page, founder of Google, is obsessed with speed. "Before Google launched Gmail in 2004, its creator, Paul Buchheit, brought it to Page's open cubicle office for a review," Nicholas Carlson wrote for Business Insider in 2014. "As Buchheit called the program up on Page's computer, the boss made a face.

"It's too slow," Page said.

Buchheit disagreed. "It was loading just fine," he said.

"No," Page insisted. It had taken a full 600 milliseconds for the page to load.

"You can't know that," Buchheit said. But when he got back to his office, he looked up the server logs. It had taken exactly 600 milliseconds for Gmail to load. This is why Larry Page is so successful: he understands the preciousness of time—to the customer!

"We had a similar experience at Amazon.com," Greg Linden of Amazon states. "In A/B tests, we tried delaying the page in increments of 100 milliseconds and found that even very small delays would result in substantial and costly drops in revenue." Amazon is absolutely obsessed with reducing page loads and delivery times because it knows that this is the culture of "I want it now!" When Amazon founder and Washington Post owner Jeff Bezos "received an email from a reader complaining about the time it took for the mobile app to load, he immediately fired off a note to the newspaper's chief information officer," Lukas Alpert and Jack Marshall wrote for the Wall Street Journal in 2015. "The message was simple: fix it." The programmers got back to him and said they could maybe reduce the load time to two seconds. "It needs to be milliseconds," was Bezos' reply.

A primary responsibility for you will be managing the time of your customer. The more quickly your customers are able to complete their tasks, the more value you will create. Thus, you will need to measure customer time and the Task Performance Indicator will show you how to do that.

Be honest and transparent

When the 2007 financial crisis hit, the demand for home swimming pools plummeted. In Northern Virginia, River Pools and Spas was in deep trouble. By early 2009, orders were down from an average of six a month to less than two. Lots of people who had made orders were cancelling.

River Pools slashed its $250,000 advertising budget by 90% and focused its energies on its website with a radical strategy: answering customers' most important questions (top tasks). "As a result," according to a New York Times article in 2013, "River Pools has recovered to exceed its peak pre-2007 revenue." When the Times asked co-owner, Marcus Sheridan how they had

> What's the hottest new craze in marketing? Telling the truth.

managed such an amazing turnaround, his answer was simple. "I just started thinking more about the way I use the Internet," he said. "Most of the time when

I type in a search, I'm looking for an answer to a specific question. The problem in my industry, and a lot of industries, is you don't get a lot of great search results because most businesses don't want to give answers; they want to talk about their company. So I realized that if I was willing to answer all these questions that people have about fiberglass pools, we might have a chance to pull this out."

Marcus answered heretical questions such as:

- How much does a pool cost?
- What are the major problems and issues with fiber glass pools?
- How can I install it myself?
- Who are the competitors?

Pricing, troubleshooting, installation, competitors; these are classic customer tasks. In the chapter on customer task identification, I will give you a detailed method for assembling a comprehensive list of these tasks, and then getting customers to vote on this list, so as to identify the top tasks and the tiny tasks.

Let's say Domino's Pizza was described to you as "cardboard; mass produced, boring, bland." How would you react? Let's say these statements were made in a series of advertisements by Domino's starting in 2009. What would you think? AdAge was not impressed. "Domino's does itself a disservice by coming clean about its pizza," it complained. Can't have that, now AdAge, can we? Wow, truth in advertising, what a scary concept.

People are tired of being talked at, marketed at, advertised at.

In 2010, Dominos U.S. sales were up for the first time since 2007. Between 2010 and 2015, its stock price grew at a phenomenal rate, going from $13 to $104, a 650% return on investment. "People are tired of companies talking at them instead of with them," Patrick Doyle, the CEO of Domino's, told TIME magazine. "The old rule of thumb for companies used to be that for every complaint you hear, people are telling 10 other people. Well, those were the days when people were having one-on-one communications. Brands, because of their big marketing budgets, could overwhelm consumers with the volume of their message. Now, if a customer has a bad experience, it's immediately on Facebook or Twitter. Hundreds or thousands of people hear about it. You've got to adapt and understand that's the dynamic out there. It's pretty powerful."

Yes, it is a powerful dynamic. And the opportunities are very significant for those organizations who can embrace the new model of truthfulness, service, ease-of-use and speed. Those that can't will have to deal with the Millennial Attitude.

References

Tranquada, F. et al. *Science and the Usability Specialist: Recent Research Findings You Might Have Missed*
http://www.measuringux.com/presentations/LatestResearch/LatestResearch-Slides.pdf

Loosemore, T. *One Link on GOV.UK – 350,000 More Organ Donors,* Mar. 2014
https://gds.blog.gov.uk/2014/03/18/organ-donor-register/

Parmenter, S. *Facebook Hairdresser Study*
http://www.sazzy.co.uk

Temkin, B. *Tech Vendors Earn Loyalty by Being Easy to Work with, Customer Experience Matters,* Nov. 2013
https://experiencematters.wordpress.com/2013/11/22/tech-vendors-earn-loyalty-by-being-easy-to-work-with/

Statistic Brain. *Attention Spam Statistics,* National Center for Biotechnology Information, U.S. National Library of Medicine, The Associated Press, Apr. 2015
http://www.statisticbrain.com/attention-span-statistics/

Matthew D. et al. *The Effortless Experience: Conquering the New Battleground for Customer Loyalty,* Your Coach in a Box, Mar. 2014
https://www.goodreads.com/book/show/17924011-the-effortless-experience

CMO Council. *The Content Connection to Vendor Selection,* Chief Marketing Officer (CMO) Council, Mar. 2014
https://www.cmocouncil.org/download-center.php?id=278

Binch, W. *Advertisers Must Be Inventors,* Harvard Business Review, Feb. 2013
https://hbr.org/2013/02/advertisers-must-be-inventors

Sterling, G. *Massive Exposure, Minimal Impact: Doubts about Super Bowl Ad Effectiveness.* Surveys and Sales Data Show Limited or No Benefit from Super Bowl Ads, Marketing Land, Jan. 2015
http://marketingland.com/massive-exposure-minimal-impact-doubts-super-bowl-ad-effectiveness-116572

Walden, S. *Southwest CMO Kevin Krone on the Future of Marketing,* Mashable, Mar. 2015
http://mashable.com/2015/03/24/southwest-cmo/#a2yUCrorIkqi

Newitz, A. *Almost None of the Women in the Ashley Madison Database Ever Used the Site* [Updated], Gizmodo, Aug. 2015
http://gizmodo.com/almost-none-of-the-women-in-the-ashley-madison-database-1725558944

Wilson, B. Swindled. *From Poison Sweets to Counterfeit Coffee – The Dark History of the Food Cheats,* John Murray Publisher, London, 2008.

Manjoo, F. *Google, Mighty Now, But Not Forever,* The New York Times, Feb. 2015
http://www.nytimes.com/2015/02/12/technology/personaltech/googles-time-at-the-top-may-be-nearing-its-end.html?_r=0

Bixby J. 4 *Awesome Slides Showing How Page Speed Correlates to Business Metrics at Walmart.com,* Feb. 2012
http://www.webperformancetoday.com/2012/02/28/4-awesome-slides-showing-how-page-speed-correlates-to-business-metrics-at-walmart-com/

Cutler, B. F*irefox & Page Load Speed – Part II, Blog of Matters,* Apr. 2010
https://blog.mozilla.org/metrics/2010/04/05/firefox-page-load-speed-%E2%80%93-part-ii/

Brutlag, J. *Speed matters (Google research on page download times),* Google Research Blog, June 2009
http://googleresearch.blogspot.ie/2009/06/speed-matters.html

Shurman, E. & Brutlag, J. *Performance Related Changes and their User Impact* (Google and Bing page download study).
http://assets.en.oreilly.com/1/event/29/The%20User%20and%20Business%20Impact%20of%20Server%20Delays,%20Additional%20Bytes,%20and%20HTTP%20Chunking%20in%20Web%20Search%20Presentation.pptx

Schrage, M. *Why Your Customer Loyalty Program isn't Working,* Harvard Business Review, Mar. 2015
https://hbr.org/2015/03/why-your-customer-loyalty-program-isnt-working

Corporate Executive Board. *Consumers Crave Simplicity Not Engagement,* May 2012
https://news.cebglobal.com/press-releases?item=128138

Dixon, M., Toman, N. & DeLisi, R. *The Effortless Experience: Conquering the New Battleground for Customer Loyalty,* Your Coach in a Box, Mar. 2014

Shah, D. *STOP! Before You Add That Feature, Do You Know the Real Cost?* Feb. 2013
http://product.hubspot.com/blog/stop-before-you-add-that-feature-do-you-know-the-real-cost

Carlson, N. *The Untold Story of Larry Page's Incredible Comeback,* Business Insider, Apr. 2014
http://uk.businessinsider.com/larry-page-the-untold-story-2014-4?r=US&IR=T

Linden, G. *Geeking with Greg: Marissa Mayer at Web 2.0,* Nov. 2006
http://glinden.blogspot.ie/2006/11/marissa-mayer-at-web-20.html

Alpert Lukas I. & Marshal J. *Bezos Takes Hands-On Role at Washington Post,* The Wall Street Journal, Dec. 2015
http://www.wsj.com/articles/bezos-takes-hands-on-role-at-washington-post-1450658089

Cohen M. *A Revolutionary Marketing Strategy: Answer Customers' Questions,* Feb. 2013
http://www.nytimes.com/2013/02/28/business/smallbusiness/increasing-sales-by-answering-customers-questions.html?_r=2&

Garfield, B. *Domino's Does Itself a Disservice by Coming Clean about Its Pizza. We Like Apologies and Honesty, But There Are Limits. Just Ask Ford,* Jan. 2010
http://adage.com/article/ad-review/advertising-domino-s-a-disservice-ads/141393/

Gregory S. *Domino's New Recipe: (Brutal) Truth in Advertising,* May 2011
http://content.time.com/time/business/article/0,8599,2069766,00.html

8
MILLENNIAL ATTITUDE

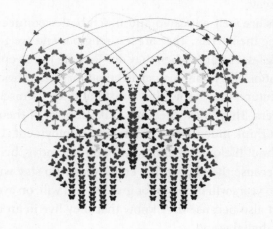

Millennial Attitude
Flexible and in control

More than anything, Millennials—those born from the early 1980s to early 2000s—want control of their lives, so build the tools that give them control. Millennial is not simply a generation. It is an attitude that is reaching across generations. Millennials are poorer than their parents' generation. In the US, Millennials wages actually fell across a range of industries between 2007 and 2013. This was particularly the case in retail and hospitality, where wages dropped by an average of 10% and 16%, according to the US Census Current Population Survey.

Millennials are well-educated and much better connected. They feel powerful among themselves. They are less religious and are getting married later and having less children when they do. They are just as optimistic as any previous generation. They don't look up to brands or institutions or figureheads as much. The future, they know, they must build for themselves with their friends and peers. They know they must take control of their own careers. That they must think independently. Lifelong employment is a fairytale for them. It's all about lifelong learning, being on the move, being in control. That's partly because they know that employees who stay with companies longer than two years will be taken for granted and will, on average, get paid 50% less, but it also because they know that they live in an impermanent, ever-changing digital world.

Millennials aren't taking or buying crap

Millennials value privacy and many of them see Edward Snowden as a hero, according to a 2015 poll by the American Civil Liberties Union. A 2014 poll by the Harvard's Institute of Politics found that "cynicism toward the political process has never been higher. It's been clear for some time now that young people are growing more disillusioned and disconnected from Washington," said Harvard Institute of Politics Polling Director John Della Volpe. "There's an erosion of trust in the individuals and institutions that make government work."

The core message here is that the customer has radically changed. We can't do as much old model design that's focused on huge beautiful visuals and images of actors pretending to be customers, and gushing content that talks about how much the organization cares and how easy they are making things for customers. There is no blind trust with Millennials. They'll try and use the thing you've designed, and if it's not fast and easy … Next!

Millennials would prefer to clean a toilet than ring customer service. They want to do things for themselves because often when they interact with organization employees they have to wait ages, and often they don't even get their problems solved. "Millennials aren't buying crap anymore, destroying businesses that, well, sell crap," Danny Crichton, a millennial, wrote for TechCrunch in 2015. "I want to transfer money in ten seconds – not ten screens. Along that simplicity theme, part of shedding all of these human touch points is also reducing the complexity of banking products. Every time I go to a bank, there is a rigmarole involved as we go through the new-account-type-of-the-month, each of course with their complex tiers of fees. I know this is designed to screw me, and I don't like it. Simplicity is golden."

Are you working for an organization that "sells crap" or that treats its current customers like crap? It's going to get harder. So, you need to make a decision. You need to help convince your organization to do useful stuff, or else you need to find an organization that sells valuable stuff or delivers valuable services and work for them. In such an organization, you can make a real difference and build a successful career. The crap sellers did great in the old model of blind trust and mass marketing. They're not going to do nearly as well in the new model of skepticism and impatience.

> Being technology dependent does not mean being tech savvy.

Millennials "will not tolerate waiting in lines, repeating their problem to five different people or being treated like a number," Joe Gagnon and Jason Dorsey state in a 2015 survey of Millennials. "Companies that do not adapt risk obsolescence as this new generation becomes an economic powerhouse."

The disloyal generation

"Millennials are self-reliant and technology dependent, but not necessarily tech savvy, and they expect instant gratification," said Jason Dorsey, Chief Strategy Officer at The Center for Generational Kinetics. "They don't just like speed and ease of use, they expect it."

Millennials are disloyal. According to a 2014 survey on Millennials by Aspect Software, over half of them dropped at least one brand in the past twelve months because of poor customer service. A study by McCarthy found that 84% of them dislike advertising. A 2014 study on telecom providers found that Millennials were twice as likely to switch providers as any other group.

Not surprisingly, Millennials are cost conscious. They "are less interested in name brands and more about creating their own unique style," Washington Post wrote in 2015. "They're also less willing to pump their entire paycheck into their wardrobes." Millennials want to create a unique look and do it at a lower cost. Abercrombie & Fitch, for example, the teen retailer, who made fat profits by getting teens to pay to advertise their products by walking around with huge A&F logos emblazoned on their chests, was forced to go logo free in 2014 because Millennials sneered at the idea of paying to be a human billboard.

Millennials are about finding rather than remembering. Their smartphone is their second brain, and their most valuable possession and the Web is their memory. They search quickly and ruthlessly. Millennials use four different devices daily and check their smartphones an average of 43 times a day, according to research from SDL. For 9 out of 10 of them the smartphone never leaves their side. Almost 80% reach for their phone to fill any pauses or gaps or moments of inactivity. Only 10% of those over the age of 65 do the same.

Seeking work life balance

Millennials are the least-engaged entity within the US workforce. In 2014, only 29% felt engaged by their jobs. So, 70% of millennials do not feel that they are in the right job environment. Maybe one reason for that is because, according to Forbes, "44% of college graduated Millennials are stuck in low-wage, dead-end jobs, the highest rate in decades." Not surprisingly, 60% of Millennials will leave their jobs within the first 3 years, costing their employers an average of $20,000 each. They don't particularly want job security because they know it doesn't exist anymore. What they do want is the ability to train and develop and to have a work environment that reflects their life environment—with the same cool tools and ease of use.

"Close to 80 percent of millennials surveyed are part of dual-income couples in which both work full time," Brigid Schulte wrote for the Washington Post

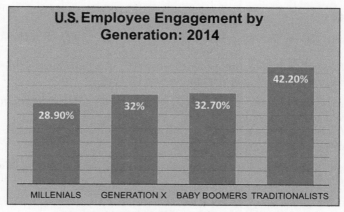

U.S. employee engagement by generation: 2014

in 2015, quoting a report from Ernst & Young. "Wanting flexibility or work-life balance is the number one thing we hear all the time from candidates," said Heidi Parsont, who runs TorchLight, a recruiting firm. "It's the number one reason why people are looking for a new job, by far. But companies still see it as making an exception. It's still not the norm."

A Pew Research Study revealed that out of the last four generations, Millennials are the first that do not place

> Lifetime employment is dead. Long live lifetime learning.

work ethic on their list of what makes them unique. It's not that Millennials don't want to work. It's that they don't want to work for "the man". They wonder why they should slave away and be loyal and obedient to organizations that shows no loyalty to them. They constantly ask "why" and they want feedback because they know they have to keep developing, keep learning, keep moving, keep connecting. According to them, their use of technology is by far the most significant thing that makes them unique. This Millennial attitude is causing a revolution in the workplace.

References

Thompson, D. *The Incredible Shrinking Incomes of Young Americans,* The Atlantic, Dec. 2014
http://www.theatlantic.com/business/archive/2014/12/millennials-arent-saving-money-because-theyre-not-making-money/383338/

Harvard IOP. *Low Midterm Turnout Likely, Conservatives More Enthusiastic, Harvard Youth Poll Finds,* 2014
http://iop.harvard.edu/low-midterm-turnout-likely-conservatives-more-enthusiastic-harvard-youth-poll-finds

Crichton D. *Millennials Are Destroying Banks, And It's the Banks' Fault,* May 2015
http://techcrunch.com/2015/05/30/millennial-banks/

Forbes. *The 5.4% Unemployment Rate Means Nothing for Millennials,* May 2015
http://www.forbes.com/sites/ashleystahl/2015/05/11/the-5-4-unemployment-rate-means-nothing-for-millennials/#4e7bef7157d4

Pew Research Center. *Millennials a Portrait of Generation Next. Confident. Connected. Open to change,* 2010
http://www.pewsocialtrends.org/files/2010/10/millennials-confident-connected-open-to-change.pdf

Aspect Software in Conjunction with the Center of Generational Kinetics. *The Aspect Consumer Experience Index study: Making It through the Millennial Customer Service,* 2015
http://www.aspect.com/millennials

Aspect Software and the Center for Generational Kinetics. *Custom Millennial Research on Customer Service Expectations,* 2015
http://genhq.com/generations-gen-y-millennials-research/millennial-research-on-customer-service-expectations/

The Aspect Consumer Experience Index. *Customer, Serve Thy Self: New Study Reveals Millennials' Desire for Self Service, Digital Interaction to Change Customer Service Forever,* Feb. 2015
http://www.aspect.com/uk/company/news-and-events/press-releases/customer-serve-thy-self-new-study-reveals-millennials-desire-for-self-service-digital-interaction-to-change-customer-service-forever

Bever, L. *How Millennial Shoppers Have Made Gap's Uniform Look Obsolete,* June 2015
https://www.washingtonpost.com/news/morning-mix/wp/2015/06/16/how-millennial-shoppers-have-made-gaps-basic-look-obsolete/

SDL. *The Future of Customer Experience: Five Truths for Tomorrow's Marketer,* 2014
http://www.sdl.com/ilp/cxc/five-future-truths/

Adkins, A. *Gallup: Majority of U.S. Employees Not Engaged Despite Gains in 2014,* 2014
http://www.gallup.com/poll/181289/majority-employees-not-engaged-despite-gains-2014.aspx

Career Advisory Board. *The Successful Independent Contractor: A Workforce Trend for the Future, 2014*
http://careeradvisoryboard.org/public/uploads/2014/06/Career-Advisory-Board-MBO-Executive-Summary_FINAL.pdf

Tyson, L. *US Jobs Data Reveals Economy Is Bouncing Back Strongly from Recession,* Oct. 2012
http://www.theguardian.com/business/2012/oct/17/us-employment-data-recession-recovery

Schulte, B. *Millennials Want a Work-Life Balance. Their Bosses Just Don't Get Why,* The Washington Post, May 2015
https://www.washingtonpost.com/local/millennials-want-a-work-life-balance-their-bosses-just-dont-get-why/2015/05/05/1859369e-f376-11e4-84a6-6d7c67c50db0_story.html

9
REVOLUTION IN THE WORKSPACE

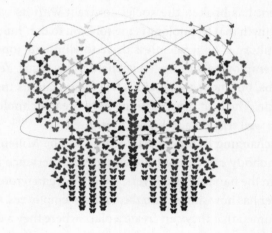

Revolution in the Workspace
Employees are not the problem

The typical workplace of today sucks. Big time. We most definitely need a new model for work. What went wrong? Technology was supposed to make our lives easier. In our personal lives, it certainly has, but when it comes to work, many of us are working longer and longer hours with horribly designed technology, and getting paid less. Stress is everywhere.

There may be a whole range of reasons for this, but at the heart of everything is that management does not value its workers. A 2015 poll by Monster.com found that almost half of US workers said they "never" feel appreciated for their hard work. Only 10% feel that they get some occasional praise from their managers. These are truly shocking figures but they are sadly typical.

Management has broken the social contract with its workforce and bought into the myth that technology is the solution to the "human" problem. Management culture is on a relentless drive to eliminate jobs and remove benefits. Those employees that are left get hardly any focus. Yes, technology does replace jobs, but there are precious few organizations that can run on technology alone. The best organizations have great technology and great people, who are well trained and highly motivated.

Things are changing though, partly driven by the Millennial Attitude. "Decades ago nobody cared about the employee experience because all of the power was in the hands of employers," Jacob Morgan wrote for Forbes in 2015. "The power has now shifted into the hands of employees. Organizations have always assumed that they can create a place where they assumed people needed to work there and are now realizing that they must create a place where people want to work there. The war for talent has never been more fierce."

Unfortunately, in the majority of organizations, the "war for talent" has not yet resulted in much improvement in the work environment. Most employees are still seen as mere incidental bit players in a game where they will be ultimately replaced by machines or outsourced to some country where people work for much less. Thus, the role of technology in organizations is not to support employees but rather to track, manage and ultimately replace them. The idea that technology should be used to help employees do their jobs faster and easier is not even something that would enter the typical senior manager's mind.

Knowledge workers think for a living. They use information to make decisions. They work with ideas. They design solutions to problems. They are the workers who are left after you've outsourced everything you can outsource and replaced as many as possible with new technology. Up until now, there has been an almost total lack of human-centered design thinking when it comes to how we use work-based technologies for these workers. Management does not care about the usability of the digital workspace of knowledge workers. They see technology as a means of management control rather than employee enablement. For the vast majority of managers this is not some malicious scheme but rather an old model mindset and culture that they have slipped into.

Because many knowledge workers are on a salary and thus don't get overtime, management feels that it can use as much of this time as it likes. This cultural mindset has resulted in unsatisfactory work environments that are highly unproductive, dispiriting and overwhelming for employees. That's all about to change.

What happened to the four day week?

"After World War II, Americans were told that if they worked hard and played by the rules, a technological utopia was just over the horizon," Matt Novak wrote for Paleofuture in 2014. When Winston Churchill was UK Prime Minister in the 1950s, he believed that advances in technology would enable society to give "the working man what he's never had – four days' work and then three days' fun."

In 1997, McKinsey wrote a visionary report about knowledge work. It estimated that even at that stage, 51% of work in the US was knowledge work. Much of the report was genuinely insightful, predicting, among other things, that banking would be seriously shaken up. However, again it fell into the trap of technology utopianism when it predicted that all this wonderful technology would ensure that "workers could do their jobs in less than half of the time they currently spend."

"The elephant in offices all around the world is that people are running on empty," Tony Schwartz wrote for The New York Times in 2015. "If you are expected to work 60 or 70 hours a week, or to stay connected in the evenings and on the weekends, or you can't take at least four weeks of vacation a year, or you don't have reasonable flexibility about when and where you work, then your company can't be a great place to work." The evidence is everywhere. For example, Adweek reported in 2015 that 80% of marketers say they are overloaded and understaffed.

Decision factories

Why with so many technological advances do we have such awful, unproductive workplaces? Bad design. Most workplace technology has technical design but very little design that is focused on making the technology easy and fast to use. Management has bought into the myth that all they need to do is pay the bill for the technology, and this has led to a world of enterprise technology that is focused on selling itself to senior management, knowing that nobody cares about how easy it is to use. So, we get technology full of features and technical prowess that is quite simply a nightmare to use.

Knowledge workers work in "decision factories". A good digital workspace should help them make faster, better decisions. "Companies everywhere struggle with the management of knowledge workers," according to Roger Martin, dean of the University of Toronto's Rotman School of Management. "Their raw materials are data, either from their own information systems or from outside providers. They produce lots of memos and presentations full of analyses and recommendations. They engage in production processes—called meetings—that convert this work to finished goods in the form of decisions. Decision factories have arguably become corporate America's largest cost.... And as China and other low-cost jurisdictions bring more and more manual workers on-stream, the developed economies will become ever more reliant on knowledge workers, whose productivity may therefore be THE management challenge of our times."

This is the challenge for the enterprise designer! To make knowledge workers the most efficient and productive they can be.

If the typical knowledge worker "factory" was organized like a traditional factory, it would be shut down. Finding the right information or the right person is a cruel joke in most organizations today. (Unless you know who to ask.) Enterprise Search is considered a critical success factor in 78% of organizations responding to a 2013 global survey by Findwise, but only 3% of respondents considered it very easy to find the information they needed using search. "Research by Atos Origin highlighted that the average employee spends 40% of their working week dealing with internal emails which add no value to the business, according to The Guardian in 2012. "In short, your colleagues only start working on anything of value from Wednesday each week."

There is an absolutely massive productivity gain to be achieved if we can create simpler, more effective digital workspaces. The way we achieve this is by focusing on employee top tasks and by measuring the outcomes of these tasks. We must measure whether employees are able to find the people and experts they need, for example, not whether we have a system for finding people. We must shift from managing inputs to managing employee outcomes.

Technology for management control

"This is going to be a very effective sales management system," I heard the IT executive state. "It will deliver so much more rich information to management."

"Okay, so the system that it replaces required a sales rep go through three steps in order enter a sales lead, and this new one has 13 steps ..." I waited for him to see the absurdity of asking busy, stressed out sales reps to go through 13 horribly designed steps, when they were used to going through just three steps. But he didn't get it. "Give them a half-day's training," was his reply. "They'll be fine." It is sad to say that this IT manager was typical of the managers I have met over 20 years of consulting on intranets.

As Bill Jensen wrote for Huffington Post in 2015, "The majority of corporate infrastructures, tools, budgeting, resourcing and reporting relationships are still corporate-centered—designed to make it simpler for the company to succeed—but usually more complex for each individual." This new 13-step lead input system was going to deliver rich data to senior managers that would help them much more easily control their sales reps. The sales reps were essentially being asked to work harder so that they could be micromanaged more. Classic old model thinking.

In our personal lives, we control the technologies, we use them and they are there to serve us. In our work lives, it can often seem that the technologies are there to control us, that they are imposed on us. Not only are they horrible to use but the purpose of the information that we put into them is often so that management can have more control over what we are doing.

Employees are beginning to revolt. In 2013, for example, Avon cancelled a $125 million investment in a SAP enterprise system that had taken 4 years of effort to install. Basically, Avon sales people refused to use it because it was a usability nightmare. A 2013 study by Merkle Group found that 63% of these sales management projects failed. Numerous other studies show that up to 70% of IT projects fail. That's beyond shocking.

There is no greater testament to the failure of traditional IT than the Bring Your Own Device trend. According to IDC, the number of employees who will be bringing their own devices to work will rise from 175 million in 2014 to 328 million in 2017. The core purpose of an organization should be to organize. This is a revolt of the employees against their organizations' systems. If employees feel they must bring their own devices in order to be organized, then what is the purpose of the organization?

Organizations globally are sitting on historically high levels of cash, yet they are not investing it in order to make themselves better organized. Twenty five years ago if you told someone you worked for a large organization, they envied all your access to the coolest technology. Now, they sympathize with you. "Consumer IT spend has grown five times in a decade," Mark Hurd, Oracle CEO stated in 2015. "Companies' IT spend in that time frame is flat—and 82% of their spend is on maintenance; only 18% on innovation. Consumers are innovating. Companies are not. Companies have to keep up."

Productivity is hurting

"A decade-long global decline in productivity growth threatens future competitiveness, profitability, wages, and living standards in both mature and emerging economies," The Conference Board announced in its 2015 report on global productivity. The report was backed up by analysis from the Wall Street Journal which found productivity in the US had halved between the 1990s and the 2000s.

"A detailed analysis of different metrics since the mid-2000s shows the primary problem with productivity is not inefficient workers," said Bart van Ark, The Conference Board chief economist. "Rather, companies and countries appear increasingly unable to translate investments in technology and innovation into timely gains in output." Why? Lack of employee and customer-centered design thinking, lack of simplicity thinking, little or no focus on ease-of-use. And the wrong metrics. The old model measured the technology itself, not its use.

Focusing on use means focusing on things like findability. It means focusing on usefulness. How long did it take the sales rep to add a lead? Can we make it simpler and faster? How long does it take them to find the sales presentation for Product X? Did they have to call or email someone because they couldn't find it through search? Was it useful when they found it? Was it up-to-date? Was it the best one? Or was it one of 20 other slightly similar sales presentations for Product X that left the sales rep confused and annoyed as they opened each one trying to figure out which was the best one to use?

In most organizations, these knowledge management systems are not much more than fetid dumps of out-of-date duplicates of information that wasn't even much good to begin with. 80-90% of marketing collateral plays no useful role in the selling process, according to Andy Markowitz, from the Lead Performance Marketing Lab at GE. "Product marketing sits in an ivory tower and 'creates a promotional potpourri … of sweet smelling stuff' that is appealing to them," according to Tom Evans, CompellingPM. As a result, "sales reps spend less than one-third (32%) of their time selling and pitching prospects, according to The Huffington Post. "They spend a near-equal amount of time (31%) searching for sales collateral or creating their own branded content."

It all comes back to the old model culture of production, the cult of volume, the cult of content as ego. More and more and more. In 1997, I worked on my first intranet and since then in practically every intranet project, we have had to delete up to 90% of the content in order to make the intranet useful. That happens year-in year-out but organizations measure success based on the production of stuff, rather than on the sales rep being able to quickly find the right sales presentation. To change this culture you must test top sales tasks with real sales reps and show management what it is actually like to be a sales rep. If you're lucky, their reaction will be one of shock because it will likely be the very first time they will have seen a real sales rep actually try to do their job using the unusable systems that management bought.

Email is a classic example of a production culture. In 2013, there were over 100 billion business emails sent every day, and this is expected to rise to 130 billion by 2017. And with mobile, we can send and read 24-7, from the train, on the toilet, in bed, on top of a mountain even. A study by Apex Performance found that 70% of respondents received more than 20 emails a day. Half of them checked their email more than 11 times a day, which is about every 20 minutes. Productivity requires focus. A 2007 survey by Microsoft found that it took employees an average of 15 minutes to regain focus after they had responded to an email or phone call. It's a miracle anything gets done at all.

In a digital economy, the scarcest resource is good people and their time. Clayton Christensen believes that we have an outdated assumption that capital is the scarce resource. "But capital," he explains, "is no longer in short supply—witness the $1.6 trillion in cash on corporate balance sheets—and, if companies want to maximize returns on it, they must stop behaving as if it were. We would contend that the ability to attract talent, and the processes and resolve to deploy it against growth opportunities, are far harder to come by than cash." A 2015 study by IDT found that the organizations surveyed felt that only 27% of their business executives possessed the technology skills necessary for digital transformation, while only 39% said they had the skills required to manage Big Data. Despite this skills gap, only 10% of the respondents said that they had recruitment / training programs in place to close the skill gap.

So, we're still at a scary moment. While organizations recognize that digital transformation is essential, a great many of them are not at all prepared for this challenges that transformation throws up. Thus, they are more likely to face extinction rather than transformation. You need to evaluate your organization on an ongoing basis.

New model organizations will focus on creating the simplest, fastest and most useful possible environment for the knowledge worker. These are the people who will make the digital transformation a reality. We must make the best use of their time. We must become obsessed with optimizing knowledge worker time—from the point of view of the knowledge worker!

In the Nineties (before Google maps!), I consulted for a very large global organization that had multiple locations, even in the same city. Finding an office or factory building was no easy task. There were countless maps and directions, much of them badly designed and out of date. We tested some "find a location" tasks and discovered that it took an average of 4 minutes to find a particular location. With a new design, ongoing management and a focus on simplicity, we estimated that we could reduce the time to find a location from 4 minutes to 1. There were 10,000 find a location requests every month.

When I presented this to a senior manager, he just shrugged. "Three minutes? They could be out smoking a cigarette."

"Yes," was my reply. "They could. But right now, these three minutes are lost. If we simplify, you get the three minutes back. It's then up to you to use it productively." He smiled at my innocence.

"These are just soft metrics," he stated. "Tell me how many people I can fire after you save these minutes. Then I'm interested."

Employees are fighting back

"The 80-hour work week is a sham," Bloomberg wrote in 2015, "A recent study outed a group of people, mostly men, who play the part of the workaholic, feigning brutal hours, while covertly keeping a more humane schedule." Only a total idiot would actually work an 80 hour week every week. People know they're being exploited and are finding subtle ways to fight back. "The workplace is where people go to work," Peter Fleming, of City University London, writes for the BBC. "But much of the day is increasingly padded out with less productive activities."

This macho culture of putting in the hours is draining our productivity and creativity. Maybe it can work for a while in messianic companies like Amazon, who seem to attract extreme high achievers, who get a thrill out of burning themselves and their co-workers out, but in the long-term this testosterone-soaked landscape is poisonous to all but the workaholics.

"I wanted to introduce you to the 10 Power Commandments," a leaked note to interns from an analyst at Barclays' financial group stated. "We expect you to be the last ones to leave every night, no matter what ... I recommend bringing a pillow to the office ... Play time is over and it's time to buckle up." Is this exceptional? Not really. Bank of America intern, Moritz Erhardt died in 2013 as a result of an epileptic seizure after working 72 hours straight. He obviously wasn't management material. And we wonder why management lacks empathy? And we wonder why financial institutions drove us over a cliff in 2007? Not surprisingly, "the incidence of psychopathy among CEOs is about 4 percent, four times what it is in the population at large," according to Forbes.

Now, I know you're thinking: I can't change any of this. Yes you can. Behave like a Millennial. Ask why? Switch. Switch brands. Switch jobs. The foundation of the old model is built on our apathy and loyalty. Don't accept these ridiculous working conditions. Find others who agree with you because all around you people are thinking: "This is a crazy way to have to work." If the revolution in the workspace is to gain momentum, it must start with people like you. It certainly is highly unlikely to start at higher-up levels because the old model helps them rake in the mega salaries and bonuses.

Disengaged, overwhelmed employees

This is the age of disengagement at work. According to Gallup, in 2014 almost 70% of US employees felt disengaged with their jobs. Worldwide, Gallup estimates that 87% of employees are not engaged at work. Companies lose $350 billion a year because of employee disengagement, according to Dale Carnegie Training.

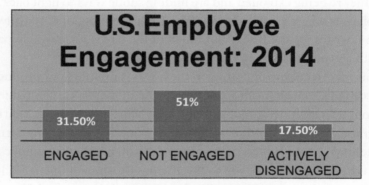

U.S. employee engagement: 2014

Two-third of employees feel "overwhelmed," according to a 2014 Deloitte Global Human Capital Trends survey of 2,500 organizations in 90 countries. 70% of people say that they would describe themselves as "happy" in their personal lives when interviewed for a Future of Work survey. However, only 29% agreed with the statement, "I can achieve my dreams and goals where I currently work." A 2015 Workboard survey found that "disengagement abounds, as 87 percent of employees are not inspired to achieve goals, and 93 percent of employees can't relate company goals to their everyday actions."

Management disconnect

A 2014 Towers Watson Global Workforce Study of US employees found that 45% do not trust senior management, and do not believe they provide effective leadership. In 2014, Harvard Business Review found that half of employees don't feel respected by their bosses. In the same year, Forbes found that employees who stay in companies longer than two years get paid 50% less than those who switch. Yes, you read that right: the more loyal you are, the less you get paid.

53% of CEOs admitted, in a 2014 Teradata survey, that their employees don't have access to the information they need to do their jobs well. That's a pretty scary number. What is the purpose of management if not to provide employees with the information to do their jobs?

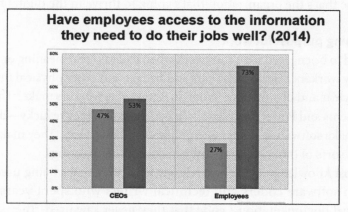

Have employees access to the information they need to do their jobs well? (2014)

Employee access to information: 2014

However, an even scarier number arises when they asked employees. 73% said they didn't have the right information to do their jobs. "CEOs are convinced that their organizations are doing a far better job with data analytics than they actually are," the survey authors stated. Your rebel mission is to bring the experience of employees to management. Have them see first-hand what it's actually like to work in the organization.

A Chartered Institute of Personnel and Development survey in 2012 found that more respondents felt trust between management and employees was weak, rather than strong. However, as you went up the management chain, the feeling was that trust between management and employees was okay.

Today, 80% of Millennials are dual-income couples, while only 47% of top management are part of a dual income family, according to a report from Ernst & Young. "I really see that there's an empathy gap in the workplace," Karyn Twaronite from Ernst & Young told the Washington Post. "When there's frustration about work-life balance in the workplace, and you think your boss doesn't get it, that very likely could be true."

The old model organization is hierarchical and disconnected. Management lives in a different world and interacts with employees through reports and screens. Very little empathy flows downward. If you work in such an environment, you don't have to. There is a global skills shortage for people like you. Switch. Find a new model organization where management actually cares about employees and customers, where leadership is a collaborative process. Because that's the organization that's going to thrive in the digital future.

Designing purposeful work

It's hard to be engaged with your work when it has no real meaning or purpose. Factory workers at least make cars and fridges and other physical things that have a clear and obvious use. What do knowledge workers make? They make documents and PowerPoints and web pages—and if they're lucky—decisions. They make software and apps and graphics and interfaces. They make emails, and all sorts of other content. They make endless meetings.

Most knowledge workers rarely see what they make being used. I have known software coders and technical writers who spent years writing technical documentation / code that they never saw used. They saw their job as producing stuff. This lack of feedback is a classic symptom of the old model silo organization. The result is a debilitating, purposeless environment.

I once worked with a large intranet which contained a substantial amount of policies. We tested real policy tasks with real employees. They struggled to find the policies but even worse when they found them, most didn't understand them. They misinterpreted them, left with the wrong answer. When we presented the results, the policy writers stared at us. One of them said: "Why are you telling us this. We just write the policies." For this lady, there was no connection between the writing of the policy and its readability and usefulness. Once she published a policy, she could tick the "compliant" box and that was her job done, as far as she was concerned. And as far as the organization was concerned too. We could not find anyone in this large organization who actually felt it was their job to ensure that employees actually understood the policies. Nobody cared.

Some years later, we went through a continuous improvement testing process for policies at another large organization. One particular area moved from an initial 30% success rate to an 80% success rate after lots of work simplifying the navigation and content. When we presented the results, there was a spontaneous round of applause from everyone in the room. And the employees involved in the rewriting beamed with satisfaction. They had worked hard but they could see a result. They were helping employees solve problems. One of them told me that, in all the years she had worked with the company, this was the first time she had got useful feedback for her work.

The Web is the bridge between production and use. If we focus on use, and reward things that are easy to use, then we encourage purposeful work. Without feedback, life dies. Without feedback, work dies. Your organization desperately needs feedback pipes to be installed. Pipes that connect producer and consumer. You may not be able to solve the management disconnect problem, but you can help lay these feedback pipes, and that is a major start towards the new model. Positive feedback is more important than negative feedback. Tell employees about how what they did:

1. Increased the success rate for a task.
2. Reduced the time it took to complete a task.

Publisher saves time, visitor spends time

Old model organizations measure within the silo / department. A new model organization measures the impact the silo has on the network. In the old silo-based departmental model, the organization manages the time of the departmental employee, and ignores the time of the other employees outside a particular department.

For years, Tetra Pak has shown the slide on the preceding page to people who want to publish content on its intranet. If the publisher does things in a hurry and saves a document as a PDF and doesn't bother adding any metadata, then it will only take 10 minutes to publish. However, it will take employees 60 minutes to find and properly understand this document. In the preceding example, 310 minutes of Tetra Pak time have been consumed. This is the standard management approach for an old model organization.

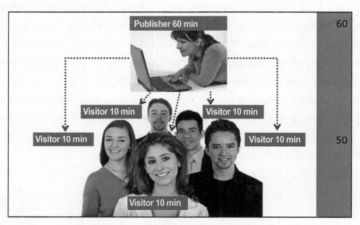

Publisher spends time, visitor saves time

However, if the publisher takes 60 minutes and edits the document appropriately, publishes as HTML and adds useful metadata, then it will only take 10 minutes for the employees to find and understand. 110 minutes of Tetra Pak time have been consumed. It's a no brainer, isn't it? The publisher should spend 60 minutes.

Except that this is totally not the case in the vast majority of organizations because they use the metrics of production rather than the metrics of consumption, and they measure the silo, not the organization as a whole. The publisher exists within a silo / department. Their time is being measured.

They are asked why they are spending 10 minutes. Can they not do it within 5 minutes? The faster they do it the better. Because their cost is part of a budget.

The visitors' / employees' time is not measured—the person who exists outside the silo and needs to consume the content. Nobody is responsible for the time of other employees who are trying to find and use this content. Nobody feels responsible for those 30 hours a month the sales rep spend searching for presentations, and then, in frustration, making up their own. This is why productivity is not growing at the rate it should. We must ditch the old model where we only measured production. It is simply not fit for purpose anymore. We must embrace the new model that focuses on use. Focusing on use will transform the workplace.

References

The Enterprise Search and Findability survey 2013
http://www.slideshare.net/findwise/enterprise-search-and-findability-survey-2013

Atkin N. *40% of Staff Time Is Wasted on Reading Internal Emails,* The Guardian, Dec. 2012
http://www.theguardian.com/housing-network/2012/dec/17/ban-staff-email-halton-housing-trust

Wong D. *Simplifying Sales: How Inside Sales Reps Can Shave at Least 15 Hours off Their Work Week,* Huffington Post, Jan. 2016
http://www.huffingtonpost.com/danny-wong/simplifying-sales-how-ins_b_8976476.html

CIPD. *Where has all the trust gone,* CIPD, 2012
https://www.cipd.co.uk/binaries/where-has-all-the-trust-gone_2012-sop.pdf

BBC Capital. *Feeling Un-Loved at Work? You're Not Alone,* Sept. 2015
http://www.bbc.com/capital/story/20150904-feel-unappreciated-at-work-youre-not-alone

Morgan, J. *Why the Future of Work Is All About the Employee Experience,* Forbes, May 2015
http://www.forbes.com/sites/jacobmorgan/2015/05/27/why-the-future-of-work-is-all-about-the-employee-experience/#6a5434112cde

Novak, M. *Paleofuture: The Late Great American Promise of Less Work,* Oct. 2014
http://paleofuture.gizmodo.com/the-late-great-american-promise-of-less-work-1561753129

Butler, P. et al. *A Revolution in Interaction,* McKinsey and Company, Feb. 1997
http://www.mckinsey.com/business-functions/strategy-and-corporate-finance/our-insights/a-revolution-in-interaction

Teradata. *The Virtuous Circle of Data: Engaging Employees in Data and Transforming Your Business,* 2014
http://www.teradata.com/Resources/White-Papers/The-Virtuous-Circle-Of-Data/

Schwartz, T. *When Employee Engagement Turns into Employee Burnout,* the New York Times, Mar. 2015
http://www.nytimes.com/2015/03/14/business/dealbook/when-employee-engagement-turns-into-employee-burnout.html?_r=0

Gianatasio, D. *Adweek: 80% of Marketers Say They Are Overloaded and Understaffed,* Aug. 2015
http://www.adweek.com/news/advertising-branding/80-marketers-say-they-are-overloaded-and-understaffed-166339

Martin, L. R. *Rethinking the Decision Factory,* Harvard Business Review, Oct. 2013
https://hbr.org/2013/10/rethinking-the-decision-factory/ar/pr

Jensen, B. *Our Relationship with Companies Must Change,* Huffpost Business, Oct. 2015
http://www.huffingtonpost.com/great-work-cultures/our-relationship-with-com_b_6836316.html

Henschen, D. *Avon Pulls Plug on $125 Million SAP Project,* Dec. 2013
http://www.informationweek.com/software/enterprise-applications/avon-pulls-plug-on-$125-million-sap-project/d/d-id/1113061

Merkle. *Merkle Executive Survey: Effective Customer Relationship Marketing Drives High-Growth Performance,* July 2013

Hamblen M. *Mobile Security: With BYOD Smartphones on the Rise, IT Headaches Will Become Migraines,* 2014
http://resources.idgenterprise.com/original/AST-0111288_mobile_sec_update-marble_v7.pdf

Harrist, M. *Why Most Customer Experience Improvement Efforts Fail,* Forbes, Apr. 2015
http://www.forbes.com/sites/oracle/2015/04/09/why-most-customer-experience-improvement-efforts-fail/#68041d8b682f

The Conference Board. *Global Productivity: Drifting into Crisis,* June 2015
https://www.conference-board.org/press/pressdetail.cfm?pressid=5479

Evans, T. *How to Create Effective Sales & Marketing Tools That Actually Get Used By Sales and Prospects!* Oct. 2013
http://www.slideshare.net/aipmm/ow-to-create-effective-sales-marketing-tools-that-actually-get-used-by-sales-and-prospects

Christensen, M. & Bever Van D. *The capitalist's Dilemma,* Harvard Business Review, June 2014
https://hbr.org/2014/06/the-capitalists-dilemma

Hoberg, P. et al. *Skills for Digital Transformation Research Report 2015*, 2015
https://www.i17.in.tum.de/fileadmin/w00btn/www/IDT_Skill_Report_2015.pdf

Greenfield, R. *Go Ahead, Fake Your Way through the 80-Hour Work Week,* May 2015
http://www.bloomberg.com/news/articles/2015-05-06/go-ahead-fake-your-way-through-the-80-hour-work-week

BBC Magazine: *Viewpoint: Why Do People Waste So Much Time at the Office?*
May 2015
http://www.bbc.com/news/magazine-32829232

Huang, D. *The Ten Commandments for Wall Street Interns,* The Wall Street Journal,
June 2015
http://blogs.wsj.com/moneybeat/2015/06/03/the-ten-commandments-for-wall-street-interns/

Ronson, J. *Why (Some) Psychopaths Make Great CEOs,* Forbes, June 2011
http://www.forbes.com/sites/jeffbercovici/2011/06/14/why-some-psychopaths-make-great-ceos/#6801bab84fac

Alcala, L. *Why Goals Fail and What You Can Do About It [Infographic],* CMS Wire
Mar. 2015
http://www.cmswire.com/cms/social-business/why-goals-fail-and-what-you-can-do-about-it-infographic-028465.php

Towers Watson. *The 2014 Global Workforce Study,* 2014
https://www.towerswatson.com/assets/jls/2014_global_workforce_study_at_a_glance_emea.pdf

Porath, C. *Half of Employees Don't Feel Respected by Their Bosses,* Nov. 2014
https://hbr.org/2014/11/half-of-employees-dont-feel-respected-by-their-bosses

Keng, C. *Employees Who Stay in Companies Longer than Two Years Get Paid 50%
Less,* June, Forbes, 2014
http://www.forbes.com/sites/cameronkeng/2014/06/22/employees-that-stay-in-companies-longer-than-2-years-get-paid-50-less/#562b7b71210e

McCafferty, D. *CEOs Unaware of Company Data Frustrations,* CIO Insight, June
2015
http://www.cioinsight.com/it-management/slideshows/ceos-unaware-of-company-data-frustrations.html

Schulte, B. *Millennials Want a Work-Life Balance. Their Bosses Just Don't Get Why.*
The Washington Post, May 2015
https://www.washingtonpost.com/local/millennials-want-a-work-life-balance-their-bosses-just-dont-get-why/2015/05/05/1859369e-f376-11e4-84a6-6d7c67c50db0_story.html

10
A MAP FOR THE DIGITAL WORKSPACE

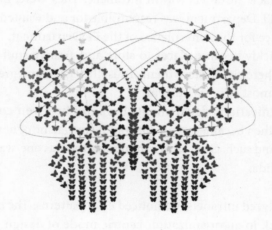

A Map for the Digital Workspace
Evolution of the digital workspace

Since 1997, my colleagues and I have been analyzing digital workplaces / intranets with a view to making them simpler to navigate and search. We noticed a clear evolutionary path:

- They began in classic silo fashion with an information architecture/ navigation mapped directly to the organizational departmental or divisional structure. If you didn't have a deep understanding of where everything fits within the organization chart, you couldn't find your way around.
- They began to include navigation labels for "Tools" or "Systems", which were in fact "intranets within intranets". They were, in essence, stuff that the IT Department was responsible for and wanted to keep in the same place for the convenience of the IT Department.
- They quickly became places to store and archive stuff because there was nowhere else to store them. Thus, they grew and grew and grew in volume, most of it not current.
- Communications departments began to be given control and the intranet then became a sprawling online magazine of new stories, press releases and such. Often, this communication was one-way management propaganda.

As we analyzed intranets, we noticed clear patterns. The ones that failed remained stuck in an organization-centric mode of design. The ones that succeeded designed around employee tasks. Between 2012 and 2015 we did an analysis of 55 intranets in the US, Canada, UK, Belgium, Holland, Sweden, Denmark, and Norway. There was a mix of government and business intranets, from medium to large organizations (10,000+ employees).

In each of these 55 intranets, we had carried out task analysis whereby we identified the top and tiny tasks of employees. We compiled almost 2,500 tasks in total, yet clear patterns became evident. The following task groups began to emerge:

1. About Me
2. Find People / Collaboration
3. About The Company

4. News
5. Policies & Procedures
6. "Core" Tasks

About Me

"About Me" is mainly the group of tasks connected with your career. In an organization-centric world, most of these tasks would be found in the HR department. In every organization that we have ever analyzed—whether public or private—there is always such a set of tasks. In a typical Top Tasks analysis, up to 50% of the top tasks could be About Me type tasks.

In some polls, we saw two clear sub-types of "About Me" tasks. Firstly, there are "Service & Support" type tasks, which make use of an internal service. For instance, "order work clothing" or "what is available for lunch at the canteen" or "get IT support for my computer". Secondly, there are "My Employment" tasks such as "what was I paid last month".

We noticed a clear hierarchy in the voting for About Me Tasks:

1. Training
2. Pay / Salary
3. Work-life balance (stress reduction, flexible working)
4. Career development (performance, appraisals)
5. Leadership development
6. Safety, health and environment
7. IT support / helpdesks
8. Job vacancies
9. Employee benefits

Regardless of the environment, the above 9 tasks kept being voted for in the same basic order. In essence, what we have here is a second-level navigation that you would get when you clicked on the About Me link.

About the Company

These tasks relate specifically to the organization itself:
- History, facts and figures
- What are your organization's published strategies and plans?
- Details about its size and location and how it's organized (although organization charts are also important in Find People & Collaboration)

Find People & Collaboration

There are two types of find people tasks:

- Find a person when you know their name. A relatively easy task to design for.
- Find an expert. This is much more challenging because often when someone is looking for an expert on the intranet they require one from a different department / silo. Very few organizations are set up to facilitate finding experts.

Collaboration is strongly linked with finding people and experts. You could possibly describe this area as the social space; the space where people go to get to know each other and to collaborate, particularly in a cross-functional manner—the way of the new model organization.

News

Employees want to know what's happening with the organization, what changes have occurred, what new products and services are being offered. Traditionally, many organizations considered that "news" was what management decided was news. However, progressive digital workplaces are tapping into most highly rated / viewed social media posts, and other employee-driven news sources. What employees want is not happy clappy propaganda but rather "news I can use". News that genuinely helps them in their day-to-day work.

Policies and procedures

The digital workplace answered crucial questions such as:

- What are the branding guidelines for putting together a brochure?
- What procedure should I follow in this situation?
- What's the policy on this?

Policies and procedures are an essential part of the digital workspace, particularly for larger organizations.

Core Tasks

Every organization has a special set of tasks that go to the core of its purpose. Rolls-Royce makes engines. IKEA makes and sells furniture. The BBC makes TV and radio programs. A department of social welfare delivers welfare services. In many organizations, a typical label for such core tasks is "Products and Services."

The core tasks are the ones where most value lies. Improving them—masking them faster and easier to find and complete—is the essence of the challenge of the enterprise designer. So, if you're wondering where the best place to start in transforming the workspace, start with the core tasks. That will get management attention because that's where the value and the future of the organization lies.

Designing a task-based architecture

Based on the previous analysis, here is what the top level of a task-based navigation can look like.

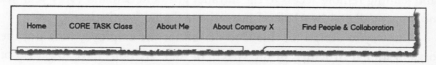

Home	CORE TASK Class	About Me	About Company X	Find People & Collaboration

Intranet / digital workspace task-based navigation

You will notice that news and policies and procedures are missing. We have found that it is more effective to associate the news and the policy with a specific task or task area. For example, on the BBC intranet if you get to the page for booking a taxi, the policy for booking the taxi is also there. If there is, for example, a change in the pension plan, this news should be available in the pension plan section of About Me. And if it's important enough then it can be promoted on the overall homepage and the About Me homepage.

In many organizations, we do a Top Tasks analysis there, we have a particular task or set of tasks that are very important to that organization. In one organization we dealt with, there was a major emphasis on training, and as a result, training was the number 1 top task for employees. There is room to add these special top tasks to the navigation.

Home	CORE TASK Class	About Me	About Company X	Find People & Collaboration	Training

Intranet / digital workspace task-based navigation

Try and keep the top level navigation with eight or less options. And, of course, you will have to name the Core Task Class. (A typical name is "Products & Services".)

From digital workplace to digital workspace

We have been doing task identification projects for intranets for more than 10 years. In all that time, the tasks have remained pretty much the same. It's been about finding people, training, pay and benefits, products and services. There has been one exception: flexible working. Every year, the need to work more flexibly gets an increased vote. Working from home hardly registered 10 years ago. Now, it is a top task for most employees. Running online meetings and gaining remote access to the intranet grows in demand every year. It's no longer a digital "workplace" but rather a digital "workspace".

The way to design for this is to design for the employee task, not the organizational structure, or the system or tool. We don't have to get rid of the organization's structures, systems and tools. We just have to make them invisible in the navigation. We need to gradually create a common interface that knits together all these disparate environments into an intuitive digital landscape, a workspace that transcends physical geography, organizational conventions and software types. We don't need one system but we do need one interface. And the way we get there is by designing for and continuously improving the top tasks.

11
COLLABORATING AND CONNECTING

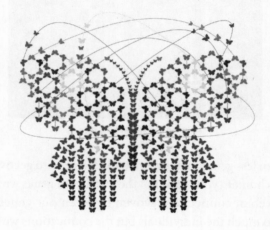

Collaborating and Connecting
What makes us human

Let's face it, humans are arrogant. We think we're just much better looking than worms. (Have you ever asked a worm what they thought of humans?) Some years ago, scientists discovered that worms had about 20,000 unique genes, and then simply assumed that humans would therefore have millions. However, according to Douglas Main, writing for Popular Science in 2014, "the estimated number has been steadily shrinking. A new study suggests that the human genome could contain as few as 19,000 protein-coding genes, fewer than nematode worms."

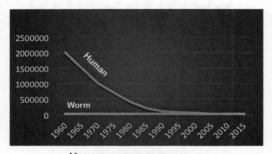

Human versus worm genes

What!? Even less genes than a nematode! No need to get overly depressed. What makes us human, you see, is not the number of genes we have but rather the complex web of connections woven between our genes. What makes society is not so much the individuals but the connections we have with each other. What makes this network we call the World Wide Web is not so much the pages and the websites and the apps, but rather the connections—the links—between everything. The magic of the Web is in the linking. It is in the connections and links where the magic of complex life resides. In a network, there are two things: the node (gene) and the links between the genes. The links get less attention and are generally more important.

In working on web stuff since 1994, here's what I have learned: We produce far too many nodes (websites, sub-sites, content, pages, apps, tools) and far too few quality links. We're not good at linking because we are trained in school to create things, not to connect things. In our observations of customers as they try to do things online, the number one reason for failure is not because of code, content or graphics, even though these do cause problems. It's because of poor quality, confusing menus and links. Linking is the art of the Web—is the art of the network—and there is no greater skill you can develop. Seriously, there is no greater skill. To have a great career in digital:

1. You will constantly be thinking about how things connect and how to connect things.
2. You will constantly be thinking of how to connect and collaborate with other people. Collaboration is messy but it is the road to success in the digital network.

In the digital network, nothing is ever finished. The physical world is about projects and endpoints but the digital world is about rapid evolution, constant learning, connecting, collaborating and evolving. The physical world is obsessed with physical things—with genes. We want more genes when we should want more connections. It used to be about how much land you had; then it became how many cows and children; then it became how many soldiers; then how many workers, how much turnover, how much sales, how many genes, how much stuff.

Digital network value is based on connections and use, not ownership. The more use you get out of it—and the more use others get out of it—the more value you create. Your value is in use, in consumption, in your network, your connections.

Thus, in digital we must focus on outcomes not inputs. It's irrelevant how many lines of code or text you write or own. Who cares if you own servers or pipes or all that physical stuff? In fact, physical often drags you down, holds you back, makes you more rigid and fixed, and less flexible and nimble. Linking and collaborating allows you to be more adaptable and nimble.

Collaboration solves complex problems

In the complex world we live in, there has never been a greater need to specialize in order to solve the problems that we face. However, specialization on its own will solve very little. Today, solving problems requires many specialists and specialisms to work together in unison in a collaborative venture.

Science is a good model for the way forward. For years, scientists have become more and more specialized in their areas of study and research. But

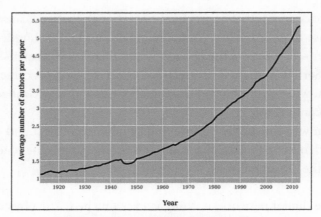

Authors per scientific paper: 1920-2010

if they are to achieve anything of worth, they must collaborate with their colleagues. In the last 100 years, the average number of authors per academic article has gone from an average of 1 to over 5. "Recent years have seen a steep increase in the number of papers with authors in excess of 50—and a particularly notable spike in reports whose author counts exceed 1,000 and more," Science Watch stated in 2012.

The mapping of the human genome was the world's largest collaborative biological project, involving multiple universities in many countries. But it was just one example of scientific collaboration. The smart people are collaborating, connecting.

Linking the internal silos

In 2013, CFO.com published a study which had asked finance professionals to comment on the following statement. "The financial data provided by operating units and subsidiaries at my company is highly accurate, requiring little correction or manual intervention." For those whose organizations that had separate systems linked by manual processes, only 26% agreed. For those with well integrated systems, 82% agreed.

Collaboration leads to greater value and higher profit, according to Heidi K. Gardner in an excellent piece of research on professional services firms entitled "When Senior Managers Won't Collaborate". When the specialists within these firms collaborated with each other, "their firms earn higher margins, inspire greater client loyalty, and gain a competitive edge," Gardner states. "But for the professionals involved, the financial benefits of collaboration accrue slowly, and other advantages are hard to quantify." Why? Because they are measured and motivated based on old model metrics. "For a firm, the financial benefits of multidisciplinary collaboration are unambiguous. Simply put, the more disciplines that are involved in a client engagement, the greater the annual average revenue the client generates," Gardner states. And yet most organizations still stick with the silo model because the silo is a known entity and is easier to manage.

The culture of silos cause the following problems:
1. Because they only think about what information they create in the context of their own silo, the navigation links and language of the content tends to be full of internal silo jargon. For example, we tested an intranet once where employees were looking for the policies in relation to "unpaid leave." They couldn't find them because HR had named the policy "sabbatical leave."
2. Duplication is rife. Organization divisions often copy HR or product information to their section of the intranet. As a result, you are likely to find multiple copies of a piece of content when you search.
3. Out-of-date content explodes. The duplicated content is rarely updated. Thus, you can find multiple copies of content, many of which are older, out-of-date versions.
4. Confusion reigns. We worked with one large organization that had multiple systems and environments for training. Employees were so confused about where to go on the intranet that they had essentially given up and were instead asking colleagues about training.

These problems must be solved by the organizations that want to survive in the new model. This transformation from silo-thinking to network thinking is at core not a systems problem but rather a cultural connecting and linking problem. Yes, buying a new software system can help but often it just compounds the problem as it becomes another silo in its own right, since the older systems are rarely shut down. Also, buying technology is often seen as the entire solution. The reason organizations have such atrocious intranets and workplaces is because they have bought awful, unusable technologies without any concern for their use. *Let's buy a new technology* is in fact one of the classic systems of the old model silo thinking.

The new model involves creating an intuitive employee-facing information architecture and navigation. (An example of which I described in the previous chapter.) It involves looking at the information itself and stripping out the jargon and making it understandable to the employees who need to use it. (Which is very different to it being understandable by those who created it.) For you to achieve these things will require you to create or become part of a collaborative cross-disciplinary and cross-silo team. All the key stakeholders in the organization must be present and the first thing on the agenda must be findability. How do we create a navigation and search that allows employees to find quickly what they need? Going hand-in-hand with findability is understandability. How do we create content / information that is easy to read and understand? These two challenges are interlinked. If, for example, an employee searches for "unpaid leave" and you change the language in the content from "sabbatical leave" to "unpaid leave", they will have a much better chance of finding and then understanding the content. It really is as simple—and as difficult—as making the language employee-centric.

Here's where the culture comes in. The silos often don't want to change the language. They feel it's dumbing down or that they're losing their specialness. The Training department wants to be called Learning & Development. You drive the change in culture with evidence of use. You test real tasks with real employees. You show that employees are searching for "training" and that they are less successful if the links are called Learning & Development.

We don't always need new software. But we do need to link up existing software with a common employee-centric interface. We might have multiple training systems, but if we can achieve a common navigation and search interface we can achieve a surprising amount. So, it's not that we must get rid of the silos, whether they be departments or systems. Once we can bridge them—link them—with a common interface, we can make them invisible. After all, people are just booking a flight or finding training. Once it's an intuitive logical flow they don't care how many systems they pass through.

When we did a customer Top Tasks analysis with the European Union (EU) in 24 languages and in 28 countries, we found that there were 77 tasks that defined what people wanted to do when interacting with the EU. When we got people to vote, we found that the top tasks were almost identical in every EU country. We also found that every single task was shared across multiple EU departments. In fact, on average each task was shared by 12 separate departments. The EU understands that it must be much more connected and it seeking create a common navigation and information architecture that brings together all aspects of a particular task into a common and intuitive interface.

In every EU country, the top tasks included law, research, funding, education, etc. There was incredible agreement and this is leading to the design of a common information architecture for the EU.

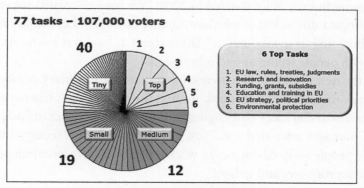

European Union citizen top tasks

When we did Top Tasks research for Cisco on their social / community web space, we found that there were two important tasks people wanted to complete: complex troubleshooting and training / career development. Engineers would come to Cisco communities and Facebook pages to ask their peers what were the best network certifications and specializations. However, once they found out the right course they then had to go back to Cisco.com and head to the Training section to find it. Linking up the environments in a logical and seamless way would provide a better experience for customers. On the Web, no website or app is an island.

Linking people

Facebook was born because Harvard University was continuously putting off creating an efficient people directory. Obviously, Harvard management didn't see it as being worth the money or effort to allow people to easily connect with each other. Not at all untypical. Most managers simply do not recognize the huge potential value of quickly, easily and accurately connecting people.

"Harvard had repeatedly said it would combine its various campus directories—what it called 'facebooks'—into one easily searchable online database," Seth Fiegerman wrote for Mashable in February 2014. Harvard continued to delay building it, so Mark Zuckerberg decided he would. So, on February 4th 2004, Facebook was born.

"The average Intel employee dumps one day a week trying to find people with the experience and expertise plus the relevant information to do their job," Laurie Buczek of Intel stated in 2009. "We have calculated some of the dollar impact due to lost productivity and opportunity. Let me just say that it is motivating us to take action." Think about it. Intel was losing one day a week with people trying to find other people.

In the new model, with network-based, cross-disciplinary collaborative and team-oriented organizations, finding the right person has never been more essential and more challenging. It used to be a lot easier to find people, a BBC manager once told me. "You just used the staff directory, but now half the people we need don't even work for the BBC. We have independent directors, producers and writers."

When I worked with Schlumberger, a large oil and gas consultancy, I was told that if the CEO gave a talk, then within hours of that talk happening, details (links to the text of the talk, video) would be made available on his Schlumberger profile. If you changed your phone number and didn't immediately update your profile, that would be seen in a very negative light. Because in Schlumberger if something breaks in an oil well, the costs per hour can be astronomical, so finding the right person as quickly as possible is essential. It's a culture of findability.

Many old model organizations have a culture of "hideability." I once asked someone why they didn't add to their profile the fact that they had just attended a conference. They looked at me and said: "I might get asked questions. More work that I don't need." I met another employee who had come up with an excellent sales presentation for a particular product. They were getting questions from other sales reps from all over the world. Their manager came to them and told them to stop answering these questions. They were being paid to meet targets within their own country, not anywhere else, they were told. Classic silo model—you only get rewarded for work that occurs within the silo.

You can't create a social workspace for a new model organization if you don't have cross-disciplinary collaboration that reaches not simply across silos, but also outside to customers and all sorts of other interested parties. And no new model organization can hope to succeed as long as old model metrics discourage and punish those who share and collaborate in a cross-disciplinary manner. You see, in most organizations the problem of findability is not primarily a technical issue. People and content don't want to get found because there is, in fact, a disincentive to get found. You get more work, which is not part of your core job. In other words, you get more unpaid, unrewarded work. It makes absolutely no sense for someone to volunteer for punishment.

We must change the model. You can't change this part of the model on your own, of course, but you can begin the conversation. When you raise the findability / "hideability" challenge, your manager will probably have never even thought about it like that. It will force them to begin to think about and address core issues. Everything begins with an idea, a thought. Everything has to start somewhere.

Leadership everywhere

The new model requires leaders everywhere, a team spirit and a collaborative environment. The hierarchical "leadership from the top" old model is broken. Its narcissistic "Great Man" culture, though, is deeply embedded. We once tested a task for a large organization's intranet, asking employees to find out about leadership development.

It was expected that employees would select the "About Me" link. (That's why it is circled in the following image.) However, far more people selected "About My Company." This was initially surprising. However, on investigation, we discovered that most employees didn't associate leadership development as being about them. It was something for an elite, for senior management, something you'd find out about in the "About My Company" section, rather than "About Me".

"How did leadership development became so elitist?" David Altman from the Center for Creative Leadership asks. "The world's challenges are big enough now that we need to think about how we can democratize

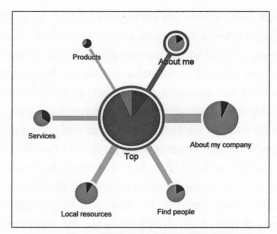

Where employees look for leadership information

leadership development, take it back to the masses—to the base and middle of the socioeconomic pyramid, not only the peak." As John P. Kotter wrote for Harvard Business Review in 2012, "People have been talking for a quarter of a century about the need for more leaders, because an organization's top two or three executives can no longer do it all."

"A new leadership paradigm seems to be emerging with an inexorable shift away from one-way, hierarchical, organization-centric communication toward two-way, network-centric, participatory, and collaborative leadership styles," Grady McGonagill and Tina Doerffer state in The Leadership Implications of the Evolving Web. "Most of all a new mind-set seems necessary, apart from new skills and knowledge. All the tools in the world will not change anything if the mind-set does not allow and support change."

A new way of leadership is on the way because the old one is simply not fit for purpose anymore. As Patrick McGovern from MIT Sloan puts it, "Some of the most important innovations of the coming decades will not be new technologies, but new ways of working together that are made possible by these new technologies." It is never safe to be a rebel, a revolutionary, but this is your time, your opportunity to be part of a major change in how organizations behave and organize.

Reinventing organizations

If you're interested in what the new model organization looks like, then you would do well to read Frederic Laloux's book, Reinventing Organizations. In it he describes the principles of these new organizational approaches.

1. **Self-management:** All business information is open to all and everyone is trusted until proven otherwise. Decision making is driven by a collective intelligence approach. Everyone has full responsibility for the organization. "If we sense that something needs to happen, we have a duty to address it."

2. **Wholeness:** Every employee is of equal worth and they are provided with a safe and caring workplace. Learning and feedback are seen as essential for growth. Conflicts and disagreements are dealt with on a one-on-one basis, but the blame culture is avoided at all costs.

2. **Purpose:** The organization has a soul and purpose. A vision is required but forecasting the future is avoided. Rather, it is essential to adapt and refine based on feedback. "In the long run, there are no trade-offs between purpose and profits. If we focus on purpose, profits will follow."

In an interview with InfoQ, Laloux describes how he "stumbled on these extraordinary organizations who have been founded (or at some point taken over) by people who believe that the organization is a living system, and that it has its own sense of direction, its own creative genius, its own thing to do in this world. And so the role of leaders (and if these organizations are self-managing, everyone can take up leadership roles) is not to make some good or bad claim to where the organizations should go. But the role of leadership is to 'listen' to where the organizations wants to go."

These new model organizations are not some utopian dream but are rather highly successful. They include:

- **Buurtzorg:** A Dutch home care organization that has 8,500 nurses who work in 800 self-managing teams of 10 to 12 people. It has purpose but no plans. It behaves like a living, adaptable system. Established in 2006, it rapidly became the leader in its marketplace in size, customer and employee satisfaction and profit.

- **ESBZ:** a publicly financed school in Berlin, covering grades seven to 12, which has attracted international attention for its innovative curriculum and organizational model.

- **FAVI:** a brass foundry in France, which produces (among other things) gearbox forks for the automotive industry, and has about 500 employees.
- **Heiligenfeld:** a 600-employee mental health hospital system, based in central Germany, which applies a holistic approach to patient care.
- **Morning Star:** a U.S.-based tomato processing company with 400 to 2,400 employees (depending on the season) and a 30 to 40 percent share of the North American market.
- **Patagonia:** a US$540 million manufacturer of climbing gear and outdoor apparel; based in California and employing 1,300 people.
- **Resources for Human Development (RHD):** a 4,000-employee nonprofit social services agency operating in 14 states in the U.S., providing services related to addiction recovery, homelessness, and mental disabilities.
- **Sounds True:** a publisher of multimedia offerings related to spirituality and personal development, with 90 employees in the United States.
- **Sun Hydraulics:** a maker of hydraulic cartridge valves and manifolds, with factories in the U.S., the U.K., Germany, and Korea employing about 900 people.
- **Holacracy:** a management system first developed at the Philadelphia-based software company Ternary, which has been adopted by a few hundred profit- and not-for-profit organizations around the world, most famously by Zappos.

Getting customer feedback

Where does the new model organization begin and where does it end? The Web makes everything diffused and interconnected. You will find that connecting with your customers will be the most important set of connections you will make. Getting feedback from and co-creating with your customers will be essential to your success. You will live in a constant world of interaction with them. Everything you do you will test with them as quickly as possible, to see if it's working, figure out what they don't like, refine and test again. A world of continuous improvement founded in the world of your customers, that is the new model in essence.

In many ways, the idea of co-creation is nothing new. How tremendously exciting it must have been when the first books started being printed. When books were written by hand they were nearly always once-offs. Thus, feedback was not very useful because it was impossible to integrate this feedback into new editions—because there really weren't any new editions. "The power which printing gives us of continually improving and correcting our Works in successive Editions, appears to me the chief advantage of that art," Scottish philosopher David Hume (1711 – 1776) is reputed to have written to his publisher.

"By the simple expedient of being honest with his readers and inviting criticism and suggestions, Abraham Ortelius (1527 – 1598) made his Theatrum atlas a sort of cooperative enterprise on an international basis," Elizabeth L. Eisenstein writes in The Printing Revolution in Early Modern Europe. "He received helpful suggestions from far and wide and cartographers stumbled over themselves to send him their latest maps of regions not covered in the Theatrum."

Print allowed for the creation of direct copies of a manuscript. Thus many people could compare and give feedback on the same thing. Print allowed for much faster publication. Thus, new editions could come out with reasonable regularity. As a result, printed maps were much easier to correct and improve than hand-created ones. "The Theatrum was…speedily reprinted several times…Suggestions for corrections and revisions kept Ortelius and his engravers busy altering plates for new editions… When Ortelius died in 1598 at least 28 editions of the atlas had been published in Latin, Dutch, German, French and Spanish." (The first edition had appeared in 1570.)

"The term 'feedback'," Eisenstein continues, "is ugly and much overused, yet it does help to define the difference between data collection before and after the communications shift. After printing, large-scale data collection did become subject to new forms of feedback which had not been possible in the age of scribes." The Web is like feedback on steroids. Big Data is a feedback avalanche. Turning all this feedback into actionable insights will be a key differentiating skill, and later—in the chapter on the Task Performance Indicator—I'll show you a simple, yet powerful, method for channeling customer feedback.

Today, Google is carrying on the same basic tradition of product evolution through feedback as Ortelius and his engravers did. Google uses multiple data sources to build the basic framework of its maps—some that it generates itself and some it gets from third-parties. Every day it receives thousands of messages from people using the maps. Where this feedback identifies specific problems with the maps, Google tries to fix these issues as quickly as possible, sometimes within minutes of receiving the feedback.

"One complaint reported that Google did not show a new roundabout that had been built in a rural part of the country," Alexis Madrigal wrote for The Atlantic in 2012. "The satellite imagery did not show the change, but a Street View car had recently driven down the street and its tracks showed the new road perfectly." An engineer began to quickly draw the new roundabout and within no time at all the change was live.

Where possible, Google gets back to people who have given feedback, thanking them and telling them about the fix. This is a really essential point. You must create a feedback virtuous circle. If you show that you are listening and acting upon feedback, you will get more of it, and of a higher quality.

This is the way forward: the road ahead.

Connect outside your comfort zone

You are a connector and your most important connections will be outside your peer group. Studies show that connections you make outside your peer group often generate more value than those within your network. It is highly unlikely you will ever drive the change you need to drive by just staying within your own network. You must combine with other skill sets because in a complex world it is cross-disciplinary collaboration that achieves success. If you are in marketing, you must work with IT, support, customer experience. If you're a content professional, you must work closely with usability and visual and software design professionals. It's all about breaking out of the silos.

We do so love our tribes, so it's not going to be easy. I remember years ago sitting in a workshop with lots of other web professionals. There was a heated and passionate discussion about the differences between information architecture, user experience, customer experience, service design, content management, web design, etc. etc. And let's not even go near software programming, branding, marketing and search engine optimization.

Sure, there are differences between these disciplines but it is the interconnections between them where the real value lies. Great web professionals are bridge builders, connectors. They don't sit within the comfort zones of their discipline telling their peers how important their particular discipline is;

how important UX, content or web design is. Instead, they go out and build bridges. I simply cannot remember a successful web environment where the techies and non-techies were not working well together.

In the new model, the old silos are becoming blurred and breaking down. It used to be that the "Support" dealt with product problems current customers had. Today, support is the new marketing. In test after test, we find potential customers going to the support section in order to find the detailed information they need to make the purchase decision. After the sale, the quality of the support will be the key determiner for many customers of whether they will buy more in the future. So, shouldn't Support, Marketing and Sales be working very closely together? Of course, they should, yet in many old model organizations, Marketing doesn't even talk to Sales, let alone Support. We need to build a lot more bridges. When Telenor Norway introduced support-type content about product installation onto their product marketing pages, their sales went up by almost 100%.

In the 2014 World Cup, Portugal had Ronaldo, Argentina had Messi, Brazil had Neymar, Uruguay had Suarez, while Germany had a team.

References

CFO Research. *Future-Proofing the Complex Modern Business: What CFOs Know about Critical Information Sharing and the Systems that Support it,* 2013
http://www.cforesearchcommunity.com/cforesearchpanel/Portals/91/Reports/Future-Proofing%20the%20Complex%20Modern%20Business.pdf

Main, D. *Humans May Have Fewer Genes than Worms,* Jan. 2014
http://www.popsci.com/article/science/humans-may-have-fewer-genes-worms

King, C. Multi-author Papers: *Onward and Upward,* Science Watch, Jun. 2012
http://archive.sciencewatch.com/newsletter/2012/201207/multiauthor_papers/

Gardner. K. H. *When Senior Managers Won't Collaborate,* Harvard Business Review, Oct. 2015
https://hbr.org/2015/03/when-senior-managers-wont-collaborate

Fiegerman, S. *It Was Just the Dumbest Luck' — Facebook's First Employees Look Back,* Mashable, Feb. 2014
http://mashable.com/2014/02/04/facebook-early-employees/#OoF0x929Nkq7

Buczek, L. *Why Intel is investing in Social Computing,* Feb. 2009
https://communities.intel.com/community/itpeernetwork/blog/2009/02/13/why-intel-is-investing-in-social-computing

Petrie, N. *White Paper: Future Trends in Leadership Development,* Center for
Creative Leadership, 2014
http://insights.ccl.org/wp-content/uploads/2015/04/futureTrends.pdf

Kotter, J. *Accelerate,* Business Harvard Review, 2012
https://hbr.org/2012/11/accelerate

McGonagill, G. & Doerffer, T. *Leadership and Web 2.0,* 2010
https://www.bertelsmann-stiftung.de/en/publications/publication/did/leadership-
and-web-20-1/

Laloux, F. *Reinventing Organizations – A Guide to Creating Organizations Inspired
by the Next Stage of Human Consciousness,* Nelson Parker, 2014

McKitterick, D. Print, *Manuscript and the Search for Order, 1450-1830,* Cambridge
University Press, 2005

Eisenstein, E. *The Printing Revolution in Early Modern Europe,* Cambridge
University Press, 2005

Madrigal, A. *How Google Builds Its Maps—and What It Means for the Future of
Everything,* Sept. 2012
http://www.theatlantic.com/technology/archive/2012/09/how-google-builds-its-
maps-and-what-it-means-for-the-future-of-everything/261913/

12
BIG DATA BUILDS RELATIONSHIPS

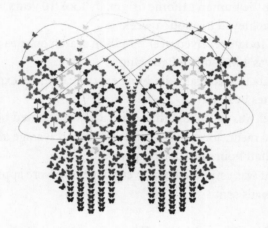

Big Data Builds Relationships
Data, data everywhere

Physical things obey the laws of scarcity. Land, oil, steel, gold are all limited resources. Digital things obey the laws of abundance. Resources such as data storage, bandwidth, networking, and processing power are becoming faster, vaster and cheaper by the day. Consider how fast the digital world is expanding and speeding up:

- Every day in 2012, 2.5 exabytes of data were created. From the dawn of civilization to 2003, about 5 exabytes of information were created.
- The world's capacity to store information has roughly doubled every 40 months since the 1980s.
- Decoding the human genome originally took 10 years to process; now it can be achieved in about a week.
- In 2012, Google received over 2 million search queries per minute. By 2014, it was 4 million and growing.
- Mobile data is practically doubling every year and is expected to reach 80 terabytes in 2016.
- By 2015, it was estimated that Americans consumed both traditional and digital media for over 1.7 trillion hours, an average of approximately 15 and a half hours per person per day.
- By 2014, it was estimated that every day there were approximately 300 billion emails sent.

Most people are fine with this. They believe that the Internet has greatly enriched their lives and allowed them access to information that helps them make better decisions. I agree. I grew up in an era when the elites and the experts controlled the flow of information. Give me the Internet any day—with all its chaos and overload—to that old model world where somebody somewhere decided what was good for us—based usually on what was good for them.

What many people are beginning to realize is that much of this Big Data is about them. We leave multitudinous digital trails everywhere we go. There is, of course, a dark and bright side to this. I'm an optimist. I believe that digital has and will continue to empower people to be more in control than they have ever been. Most of the organizations that abuse Big Data will ultimately be found out and will pay the price.

A more empowered future is not a given, though. It depends on us being active participants rather than passive consumers. (That is why it is so critical to be constantly researching, comparing and switching—it's the only way you'll keep the Big Brands honest.) The old model thrived because we were passive consumers and the longer we remain passive, the longer the old model will last. And think of this scary combination: an old model mind with access to all this Big Data on us!

In the new model, those organizations that use Big Data to enrich and simplify people's lives will reap the benefits. It won't be an easy ride. There are many battles up ahead. When people fully realize how much personal data is being collected on them, and when they see how much of this is being used to manipulate them, there will be some perfect Twitter storms, among many other storms. The right to privacy and the right to own your personal information, and the right to decide who gets to see and use your personal information will come to be established as a key human right in the new model. A Digital Rights Charter will evolve around such a basic right.

On the other side of the equation is organizational inability to manage Big Data. Yes, organizations are collecting lots of it but precious few are currently able to use it efficiently. A 2015 report by Gartner stated that 85% of Fortune 500 companies are not able to properly analyze and act on Big Data. McKinsey estimates that in the United States alone there will be a shortage of between 140,000 to 190,000 data analysts by 2018. At a basic level, data management and protection is becoming a critical challenge for organizations. Every week we hear of another major data breach, and the ones that become public knowledge are only a fraction of what's happening.

And it's only just beginning. Our phones track where we go, how many steps we take. Our watches and wristbands are monitoring our health and our exercise regimes. Our thermostats and light bulbs will record our energy consumption. Our cars will record our speed and our driving competence. Our refrigerators and cupboards will record our food consumption.

Know your customer

Digital creates a physical distance between organization and customer. It significantly reduces human-to-human relationships. You bridge that distance with data. If you know your customer well enough then you can create a design that allows them to do what they want, as easily and efficiently as possible. Good data is like a handshake, a friendly smile. Properly applied, data can show that you know what your customer likes and doesn't like. You "remember" what they bought last time, you anticipate future needs. You use their language, their words. They come to depend on you when they really need something. That's the potential of Big Data. It's huge.

Joseph Pigato has written for Entrepreneur magazine about a number of companies who truly embrace data to better serve their customers.

- **Dollar Shave Club:** Delivers razors and other personal grooming products. Relies heavily on data analytics and customer support feedback to understand their customers.
- **Etsy:** global community of craftspeople: Uses data to personalize the customer journey so as to recommend products based on factors that go beyond what people have looked at.
- **StumbleUpon:** A "discovery engine" that finds interesting content for people. Integrates data across engineering, product and marketing teams. Annie Gherini, head of marketing, notes that, "The age of departmental silos is over, and the unified efforts of all functional teams ensure that everyone is reading from the same playbook, resulting in an awesome user experience."
- **Plenty of Fish:** A dating site for 90 million people. Constant optimization through continuous testing. Agata Osinska, director of product, notes: "We are methodical about testing. You need to be disciplined about setting tests up to give you clear, accurate results."

Sam Walton founded Walmart. When his family went on vacation, they always tried to choose some rural, out-of-the-way destination. They knew from previous experience that if it was anywhere near a town or city, then Sam would disappear for long periods. They'd find him scouting around the local supermarkets, watching, observing. Once they found him on his knees as he tried to figure out the optimal height of shelves. That's the life of a customer-centric pioneer; someone who is constantly immersing themselves in the lives of their customers. Because without empathy for and understanding of your customers, all the Big Data in the world won't make much sense, or worse, you might end up using data in a way that will alienate your customers.

There is an empathy gap in the new model, and you bridge that empathy gap by being with your customers, by immersing yourself in their world. While it helps, you don't have to be physically there. In many situations, as I'll show later, it is more effective to be virtually there watching and observing them (with their permission, of course) as they go about their tasks. There is no greater skill you can develop than having an empathetic understanding of your customers as they seek to complete their tasks. Understanding how they think and how they behave online is like gold dust. It is the key that opens Big Data, and most of the other doors that matter when designing for digital.

As we'll see in the next chapter, digital design is self-service design. All the pioneers of self-service design were relentless about immersing themselves in the lives of their customers. Why? Because when people are self-serving they're running mainly on gut instinct. In self-service environments, people tend to make very fast decisions. Time becomes of the absolute essence in a self-service world. So, you must understand the customer better than they understand themselves, because when you ask a customer what they do in a particular self-service environment the answers they give are often the opposite of what they actually do when you observe them.

When Ray Kroc realized that the McDonald brothers were doing something interesting with their restaurant, he got in his car and headed out to San Bernardino. But he didn't go straight in and talk to the brothers. He parked on a hill and for two days watched intently the comings and goings of the staff and customers. He then went to the brothers and made them an offer they didn't refuse.

I once had a conversation with a McDonald's manager, who told me that one day she was in her office, her secretary was off sick and when the phone rang, she picked it up. It was her manager. The first thing she was asked was: "What are you doing in the office? Why aren't you out in the restaurant?" As a digital designer, you must imbue a culture of getting out and getting into the lives of your customers. I know this is very hard. I know that much of the culture of technology and IT—and indeed traditional design—is the exact opposite of empathy for the customer. (Design being that battle between ego and empathy.)

The first time I saw Tomer Sharon, he was working for Google as a user experience researcher. Tomer was speaking at a conference and he began taking his shirt off. Wow, I thought, haven't seen this before. Underneath his shirt was a t-shirt that read: GET OUT OF THE BUILDING. That's a philosophy and approach that is taken very seriously at Google. The first sentence of the Google design guide states: "Focus on the user and all else will follow."

So obvious for success and yet so incredibly hard for most organizations to do. "I am always amazed to find out that many people who write code have never met a person who is actually using their code," Tomer states. "When I realized that was the case with one of the teams I worked with at Google, I decided to do something about it. The idea was to get people up from their chairs and monitors and create an opportunity for them to observe and interact with real users of our products.

"Once a month, on a Friday morning, we held in-person visits at people's home or offices. We called these 'Field Fridays.'" In a typical Field Friday, a group of software engineers and I were going on a 90-minute visit to a customer home or office. The goal was to learn by observation and contextual interview as well as answering users' questions. It was extremely beneficial to both participants and stakeholders and this whole initiative was always highly appreciated by high-ups in my team."

Remember, in order to transform to the new model your number one job is to flood your organization with the experience of your customers. Because so many human-to-human touchpoints are being closed down by technology, we must open up new ones, or else the organization will know less and less about the customers who are becoming more and more important and powerful and independent.

"One thing I learned about my work is that it is extremely important to share the knowledge with team members and stakeholders who did not have a chance to join a Field Friday visit," Tomer explains. "So I launched an internal blog to which I entered posts that summarized each Field Friday event. This way, other team members learned about what happened, and had a chance to ask follow-up questions. It also raised interest in joining future events.

"Here's a quote by one software engineer who added it as a comment to a blog post published after a Field Friday visit: 'The one thing that really stood out for me was how embarrassed I was to see how bad our product was and how awkward it was for me not to be able to give good answers to any of the user's good questions.'"

Embrace flow, randomness and unpredictability

It's not important what you know today. What is important is that you know how to know or know who knows. This is a complex world and the more you know the more you realize how little you know. "If you are not completely confused by quantum mechanics, you do not understand it," the physicist John Wheeler stated. According to Nassim Taleb, in his book Fooled by Randomness, "Most results in probability are entirely counterintuitive … What sounds intelligent in a conversation or a meeting, or, particularly, in the media, is suspicious."

You must learn to embrace unpredictability and the improbable, and go with the evidence of what is actually happening. Often what you think will work, won't, and what you think won't work, will. That's perfectly okay. Adapt. Be flexible. Find the flow and go with it. Your gut instinct is a map of the past. If the map has changed, then your gut instinct can be leading you in the wrong direction. In a complex society like we live in today, the map is constantly changing, so what you require are abilities to observe, analyze the data, spot trends, test, refine, iterate.

"There are two ways to think about things," Taleb states. "Some like to know exactly what they are looking for and need to predict their environment with a lot of precision. Others accept that random events can interfere with what they are doing. The issue is that our environment is fundamentally unpredictable. At a company, not only can you not predict your own sales, you could never predict the sales of all your competitors. There are people who want to rigidly follow a map to get them through life and those that realize they need a structure that allows them to take a wrong turn and still survive. You want to turn every random event that befalls you into opportunity."

The first kind of thinker is an old model, organization-centric thinker. You must be the new model, adaptive thinker. Here's what your ideal working week looks like. On a Monday, you come up with a hypothesis of something you'd like to change in your digital world based on previous customer behavior analysis and testing. It could—and generally should be—a very small change, like perhaps changing the text in a link. On Tuesday, you put the change live and then, on Wednesday, you test with real customers to see if the change had its desired effect. Ok, so the change you made didn't work as well as expected. So, you edit the link and observe again. A continuous, never-ending process, that's how you deliver value.

Obama presidential campaign masters evidence

The Obama presidential campaigns were acknowledged masters of using the Web and in implementing a system of evidence-based decision making that flowed from a process of continuous testing.

Variations	Not Signed Up	Signed Up	Donated
DONATE NOW	0.0%	0.0%	0.0%
PLEASE DONATE	+2.3%	+27.8%	+16.3%
WHY DONATE?	-27.8%	N/A	N/A
DONATE AND GET A GIFT	+15.2%	-24.6%	+11.9%
CONTRIBUTE	+8.51	+2.9%	+18.4%

Obama campaign donation button experiment results

In the 2008 campaign, they rigorously tested the words they used for getting people to donate funds. They found, for example (as can be seen in the preceding table), that if you had not given money, then "Donate" worked well, but if you had given money at least once, then "Contribute" worked better. These word changes resulted in significant increases in donations.

In the 2012 campaign, they changed their donation page 240 times as a result of evidence they got from testing. According to Kyle Rush, former Deputy Director of Web Development for the Obama 2012 campaign, "By the end of the campaign our 240 a/b tests lifted the donation conversion rate by 49%!" And how much did they raise online? $250 million. As another Obama campaigner put it, "The time of guys sitting in a back room smoking cigars is over." This is the age of observation, of analytics, of continuous improvement, of insight and decisions based on data.

The Web is the ultimate laboratory of human behavior. Dive in. The Web is a pet scan of your customers' brain activity. This world is far too complex for any of us to predict the future, to write the perfect sentence, to design the perfect interface. We do our best to get started and then we test and tweak, test and tweak. That's how we maximize value. That's how we maximize customer satisfaction and loyalty. That's how we introduce the new model. One test at a time. One fact at a time that proves that the opinion-driven old model got it wrong again. Customer behavior is the spear point of digital change.

Fictitious names at Microsoft

At Microsoft, if you want to create some promotional content you might need to use what in legal terms are called "Fictitious Names" (John Brown, for example). But on the Microsoft intranet it used to be hard to find a list of approved fictitious names. Legally speaking, fictitious names are a type of trademark, and thus they were placed under the section "Trademarks". The web team had a feeling that this was unintuitive, but they needed evidence because without evidence they knew that they had no chance in front of the lawyers who had decided to put fictitious names under Trademarks.

So, they tested. They gave typical employees the following task: "You are looking for a person's name to use in an example in a whitepaper." Only 16% of participants were successful. The team did a bit more research in order to understand how employees thought about the task. They discovered that employees considered fictious names as a marketing task. When they placed Fictitious Names under the label Marketing, 100% of those they tested with were successful.

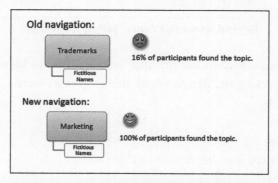

"Trademarks" versus "Marketing" navigation testing

There was some resistance from the legal experts because they felt that legally speaking they should be placed under Trademarks. However, once they saw the test results and saw how this would reduce phone calls and email inquiries, they were convinced.

Norwegian Cancer Society focuses on top tasks

The Norwegian Cancer Society, a non-profit organization, used to have lots of content on its website, much of it communicating at people, telling them that it was a non-profit organization, and that they needed to donate money if it was to continue doing its job properly. More than 45 content contributors had produced over 5,000 pages of content, resulting in a website that was poorly organized, hard to navigate, and with lots of duplicate content. In other words, it was a typical website.

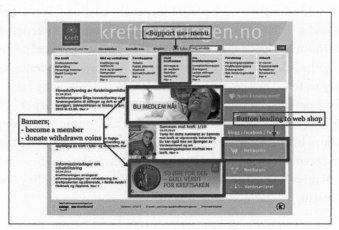

Original Norwegian Cancer Society homepage

The Society decided to use my Top Tasks method to identify customer tasks. When Norwegian citizens voted, their top tasks were:
- Treatment
- Symptoms
- Prevention

The tasks that were least important to them were:
- Donations
- Annual report
- Press releases

This is a classical organizational dilemma. The thinking goes that we can't give the citizens / customers what they want because, otherwise, we won't be able to achieve organizational / business objectives. We have a conflict here between organization needs (donations) and customer needs (symptoms, treatment). The Society did a brave and radical thing. It focused on what people needed. It followed the evidence. It overhauled its website, reducing the number of pages from 5,000 to 1,000. From 45 part-time contributors, it reduced to 6 professional editors. It created a laser focus on providing clear, simple and accurate information relating to treatment, symptoms, prevention. It deemphasized calls for donations, removing such calls almost entirely from its homepage.

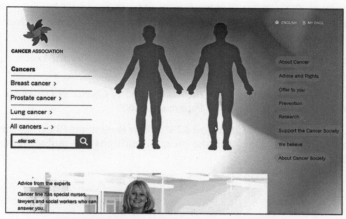

Task-based Norwegian Cancer Society homepage

What were the results?
- 70% increase in one-time donations
- 88% increase in monthly donors registered
- 164% increase in members registered
- 348% increase in incoming links
- 80% increase in visitors

What the Cancer Society did was counter-intuitive from an organization-centric, old model view of the world. It put the customer at the center. It didn't just listen to its customers. It acted on what they were saying. It built a professional, customer-centric culture. And everyone won. The customers got better, simpler information. They responded by donating more because they had experienced first-hand the value that the organization delivered. If you're useful, you'll get used.

References

Laney, D. Gartner: *Information Innovation: Innovation Key Initiative Overview,* Apr. 2012
https://www.gartner.com/doc/1991317/information-innovation-innovation-key-initiative

Manyika J. et al. *Big data: McKinsey Global Institute: The Next Frontier for Innovation, Competition, and Productivity,* May 2011
http://www.mckinsey.com/business-functions/business-technology/our-insights/big-data-the-next-frontier-for-innovation

Pigato, J. Entrepreneur: *How 9 Successful Companies Keep Their Customers,* Apr. 2015
https://www.entrepreneur.com/article/243764

Taleb, N. *Fooled by Randomness: The Hidden Role of Chance in Life and in the Markets,* Random House Trade Paperbacks, 2005

Rush, K. *Meet the Obama Campaign's $250 Million Fundraising Platform,* Nov. 2012
http://kylerush.net/blog/meet-the-obama-campaigns-250-million-fundraising-platform/

13
BUSINESS CASE FOR DIGITAL SELF-SERVICE

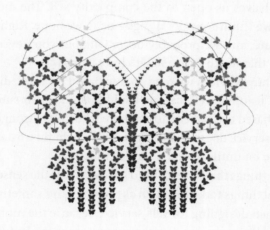

Business Case for Digital Self-Service
Digital is self-service

You must develop a deep understanding about how to design for self-service because the essence of digital is people in control of how they want to search, navigate, scan, read, and act. Humans used to deal with other humans in order to get things done. Now we increasingly deal with technology. Today, we want to do more and more for ourselves by ourselves, and we prefer signing up for services instead of buying products.

The shift to services—away from products—changes what customers expect and how they behave. Customers have never been very good at buying products, particularly complex ones. We're basically terrible at predicting the future, which leaves us open to the complexity sell. The more features we buy the more we "future-proof" things—or so we hope. Right now, we don't need that feature, and we probably never will, but you never know, and it's not costing all that much extra, so let's have it anyway.

When we buy services we tend to buy based on immediate need. If we need an extra "feature", well then we'll add that on to our subscription later. When we buy based on immediate need, we focus very strongly on simplicity and use. If the service doesn't work right now—right this instant—then many of us will move on until we find a service that does.

One of the things that attracts us to self-service is the sense of control. We want to control things today as much as possible, and sometimes that can be a challenge when designing for self-service, because the more sophisticated the controls are the more complex the environment can become. Getting the balance right will be important and you will discover where this balance lies by constantly testing with your customers.

People have an expectation that if they're serving themselves, they get some sort of reward or payback for the effort they are putting in and the effort they are saving the organization. Of course, this may be balanced by the convenience and control factor. If self-service is so much more convenient or gives you much more control, then the customer might even be willing to pay more, but that would be an exceptional situation.

There is an expectation at play here: "I'm doing all the work myself. I'm saving you money. What's in it for me?" If you are the "waiter" in a fast-food restaurant, you expect a discount. That's why McDonalds is cheap. That's why

Amazon is cheap. That's why Walmart is cheap. That's why IKEA is cheap. It's also why so much is cheap or even free in the self-service digital economy. If you want to maximize self-service uptake then you make it cheaper, faster and simpler.

Business case for digital self-service

On the surface, the digital self-service business case seems like a no-brainer. Consider the following:

- A typical banking customer call to a call center in the United States cost $7.50 in 2013. The same call handled by an overseas agent cost $2.35. If that call went through an automated self-service voice response system, it cost 32 cents. (Gallup, 2013)
- A call-out for an IT technician in the US cost an average of $797 in 2010. Dealing with such a problem over the phone cost $162. Dealing with it over the Web cost 6 cents. (Technology Services Industry Association, 2012)
- For FedEx, tracking a shipment by phone cost $2.40 in 2003. On the Web, it cost 4 cents. (FedEx, 2003)
- Dealing with a legal question on the Microsoft intranet cost $33 by phone in 2009, $10 by email and $1 using the Web. (Microsoft, 2009)
- Dealing with a typical council query in the UK cost £8.15 in 2013 for a face-to-face interaction. Over the phone, it cost £2.59, and over the Web, it cost 9 pence. (Socitm, 2013)

Based on the above figures, everything should be driven through self-service. However, it's not so simple. There is a cost to purchase and design the self-service environment, as the costs for phone and face-to-face have already been allocated. (The phones, offices, desks, etc., are already in place.) Below is a hypothetical scenario that uses an average for the cost of a task completion/ transaction in a self-service environment (web, app).

Channel	Development & Systems	Task Completion
Digital	$60,000.00	$0.40
Phone	$0.00	$6.00
Face-to-Face	$0.00	$15.00

Thus, even though the cost of a task completion is 15 times cheaper for digital self-service compared to phone and almost 40 times compared to face-to-face, there is an upfront cost of $60,000 to be accounted for.

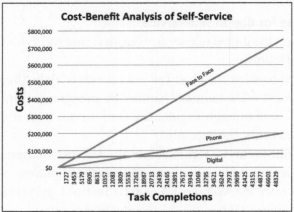

Cost-benefit analysis of self-service

Here we learn one of the most basic rules of self-service design. It needs volume. The higher the volume, the better the business case. Look at how quickly the blue line (face-to-face) increases. That's because it costs $15 for every face-to-face task completion. However, because it costs $60,000 to develop the self-service environment, we don't reach breakeven until about 4,000 task completions. Thus, for low volume—what I call "tiny tasks"—it is often a better business case to facilitate them by phone or face-to-face.

We're missing something. We're missing something big here. The above is the old model business case for self-service. Just buy the technology system and/or do some development, launch and leave. And what happens? Task failure. Self-service only works if it works. Consider the following:

- "Nearly 60% of all phone interactions saw the customer start on the company's website," according to the book, The Effortless Experience.
- When online self-service fails, 75% escalate to more expensive channels, according to Forrester.
- Success rates while using self-service on technology websites was only 51% in 2014, according to the US Technology Services Industry Association.
- In our own testing, with a large range of clients over a 10 year period, we see failure rates averaging about 40%.

Old model organizations think that it's enough to buy and install the system and that the customer will learn and adapt. That might have worked in the past but it certainly doesn't work now. Let's say John, the customer, tries to complete his task on the website and fails, and is forced to ring you. What's the cost now? It's not just $6 for the phone interaction. It's $6.40 (the digital self-service cost of 40 cent plus the phone cost of $6). Here's the dirty little secret: badly implemented self-service costs the organization more—not just in money but in the negative impacts of poor customer experiences. Poor self-service is a lose-lose situation for everyone.

So, how to we avoid that? Design and testing, of course. Ah, but that adds more cost, doesn't it? And it also adds time, so we won't be able to "launch-and-fail" as quickly as we had planned. And if it's an old model organization that manages based on organizational inputs rather than customer outcomes, then the more cost added the worse the business case becomes. If a traditional manager sees the following table, he'll go: "What? $40,000 for design and testing!? No way, José! We're not paying $100,000 for this!!! $60,000 is all we've budgeted for."

Channel	Design & Testing	Development & Systems	Task Completion
Digital	$40,000.00	$60,000.00	$0.40
Phone	$0.00	$0.00	$4.00
Face-to-Face	$0.00	$0.00	$15.00

Old model organizations just don't measure outcomes. They don't measure the cost of task failure and the cost of giving the customer a poor experience. And forget about the employee! Who cares if they have a horrible experience finding an engine diagram or a sales presentation? We're about being hardcore traditional managers here. We're about stripping away costs, not adding them.

It gets worse for the old model organization. Now, this extra element will totally blow their bean counting brains. If we want high task completion self-service, there's another cost: continuous improvement. Show them the following table and watch their expressions.

Channel	Design & Testing	Development & Systems	Continuous Improvement	Task Completion
Digital	$40,000.00	$60,000.00	$40,000.00	$0.40
Phone	$0.00	$0.00	$0.00	$4.00
Face-to-Face	$0.00	$0.00	$0.00	$15.00

"$140,000!!!! And $40,000 of that recurring every year!!!!!!! The nice software sales guy said it would only cost $60,000! That all we need to do is buy his amazing new software and then just add content and everything will be just be super-fabulous." They'll fall off their chair. They'll slump on the floor. They're about to jump up and grab you by the throat and frog march you out the door.

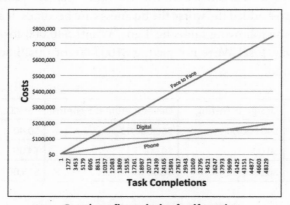

Cost-benefit analysis of self-service

Doing the right thing is a hard sell. It's a really hard sell. I know. I've been 20 years at it. It's getting better, a little easier.

The breakeven point for face-to-face versus digital has now gone from about 4,000 task completions to about 9,000. But old model managers are not thinking about task completions. They're thinking that costs have gone from $60,000 to $140,000, with $40,000 recurring every year.

You introduce the new model by stealth, because a frontal assault like the one above is bound to fail in most organizations. You begin to measure customer outcomes—task completions—and expose as many people as possible—particularly senior managers—to examples of task failures. Show them real customers trying to do real tasks—top tasks, tasks that matter—and failing, and failing again. Don't for a moment think that you will change their minds the first time you do this. I have seen it take up to 5 years for the change in culture to truly embed. And you will probably have switched jobs by then, so why bother? Because it's the right thing to do. Because even in year one, you will be able to show significant improvements. And because it will help you get a better job in a better organization that truly "gets it" and does genuinely want to manage customer outcomes. So stay optimistic, because much in the old model is managed by fear and, sometimes, the optimistic voice with compelling data can move mountains.

Not all services are suited to digital

Much of digital replaces humans with technology. For many things people want to do, that results in faster, cheaper and better experiences. But not for everything. The perfect business case for digital is self-service, where the customer does all the work on the website or app. This is both highly cost-effective and scalable. But it's not that simple. A 2015 presentation by Stefan Dieffenbacher at the UX STRAT Europe conference stated that one of Europe's largest banks found that for every minute a typical customer spent at a bank branch, they spent 99 minutes online self-serving. However, branches made nine times more sales than online.

Some services are very complex. I talked to a manager of a council / municipality who told me that services connected with planning permission were very hard to deliver online. No matter how many times they rewrote the instructions they kept getting applications full of errors and misunderstandings. So, they ended up requesting that people phone them for a 30-minute discussion before they started their planning application. Much better applications were received, saving everyone time and money in the longer term.

Think about fostering or adoption. Parents could go to a website, fill in some details and then, in a couple of weeks, a child arrives at their door. They have never met the child up to that point. Does that make sense? Not everything works for self-service and one of the greatest skills you can develop is to be able to evaluate which service—or which part of which service—works best through which channel. A task might begin on a mobile app, then move to a desktop for more extensive research, then perhaps a phone call, then back to the Web for more research and filling out of forms, and it could conclude with a face-to-face meeting.

Complex tasks that have low demand are what I called "tiny tasks." These tasks can seem innocuous but there tends to be so many of them and they also tend to produce significant quantities of content because of their complexity. The result is that they often make things harder for the simpler, high volume top tasks.

For years, Excel Function Reference content was notorious for annoying Microsoft Excel customers. Microsoft discovered that the problem was to do with keyword overlap, a very common problem caused by tiny tasks. The function pages had names like IMSUM, ADDRESS, AREAS, etc. So, when people wanted to find out how to sum a number, many of them ended up on the IMSUM function page. When people wanted to find out how to set a page area for printing, they often ended up on the AREAS function page. The solution was to delete all the function pages and put them under a single page called "Maths Functions". Satisfaction increased by 423%.

What happens with tiny tasks in most environments is that they go unmanaged and over time they make everything more and more cluttered, harder to navigate and understand. Tiny tasks feed complexity and if you want to achieve simplicity for your digital self-service initiatives, you must take great care to avoid the growth of tiny tasks.

In deciding what does and doesn't work for digital self-service, you should take the following factors into account:

1. **Online demand:** Self-service thrives on high demand: Are there lots of people who want to complete the task online? There might be lots of people who want to or need to complete the task but might not want to do it online because they feel it's not as convenient, or they feel vulnerable in some way, or they think it's just too complex. The larger the online demand the better the business case.

2. **Complexity:** Self-service loves simple tasks because when we're in self-service mode we tend to be much more impatient than when we are face-to-face with another person. The more complex the tasks, the more complex the content and app environment becomes, and the less suitable it is for self-service.

3. **Costs:** We have already looked at costs. They include:

   a. Face-to-face employee costs: How much do the employees cost who currently deliver this task, and how long on average does it take them per task completion? Look for tasks where employee time is most expensive and time consuming. (Although the cost of the employee and the length of time they need to spend helping customers complete the task in question are also likely a factor of the complexity of the task.)

   b. Development, Design, Continuous Improvement costs: How expensive is it to design and develop for the environment, and to continuously improve it? The higher the costs here, the higher the demand will be required in order to make self-service deliver value.

The following chart illustrates the "sweet spots" for the various channels when it comes to delivering quality service.

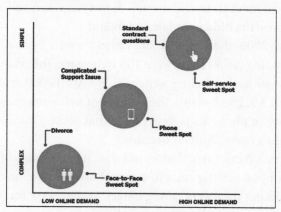

Channel sweet spots

The chart shows us that the sweet spot for self-service is where:

   a. The task is simple to complete

   b. There is high demand to do it online

   c. For example, standard contract questions on an intranet

The sweet spot for phone is where:

   a. The task is fairly complicated

   b. There is just reasonable online demand

    c. For example, a complicated support request
The sweet spot for face-to-face is where:
    a. The task is complex and has significant implications for the person
    b. There is low online demand
    c. An example might be divorce or fostering or buying a home or a
       highly complex and expensive product.

Of course, you're right to think that certain sub-tasks in an overall task such as buying a home can much more effectively be done online than in person. And this of course is where it gets interesting. In managing a particuloar task, you will need to know which channel is optimal for each step in the task.

Channel shift and hidden demand

Successful self-service causes channel shift. People move away from the more expensive channels of phone and face-to-face and use the Web. Everyone is happy, everyone saves time and money. However, when self-service works well it often unearths hidden or latent demand.

In October 2008, there were 2,202 calls to South Tyneside Council for waste and recycling tasks. There were 203 web visits. The council decided to simplify the waste and recycling webpages. By April 2009, there were 1,946 phone calls and 3,922 web visits. The number of web visits grew dramatically but the number of phone calls didn't drop that much. The simpler website had tapped into a latent, hidden demand.

I dealt with a bank once that found that when it simplified its digital services, it stopped getting calls to support about basic questions. It was getting less calls but they were taking longer, as they were more complex. So be careful not to present a business case that depends only on channel shift. Look for other scenarios where value will be created. The bank in question found that the more complex and longer-lasting "support" calls were actually turning into sales opportunities, as customers realized they needed more sophisticated services from the bank.

Hidden demand, by its nature, is difficult to predict. It is equally difficult to quantify its costs and benefits. Some customers might become information addicts, checking the stock price or weather report every hour. This sort of customer behavior may become a net cost. Other customers may start engaging more with you, and as a result buy more / do more with you. It's complicated and you need to be monitoring, measuring, getting feedback, and tweaking—basically continuously improving.

References

TSIA. *Soaring Field Service Costs Demand Investments in Process,* Technology, Technology Services Industry Association, 2012
https://www.tsia.com/resources/press-releases/2012-press-releases/2012_02_01-field_service_benchmark.html

The Economist. *Boosting productivity: On the shop floor (FedEx),* Sep. 2003
http://www.economist.com/node/2051779

Socitm. *Better with less: delivering local public services in the digital age,* Dec. 2013
http://www.socitm.net

Laney, D. *Information Innovation: Innovation Key Initiative Overview,* Gartner, Apr. 2012
https://www.gartner.com/doc/1991317/information-innovation-innovation-key-initiative

Manyika, J. et al. Big data: McKinsey Global Institute: *The Next Frontier for Innovation, Competition, and Productivity,* May 2011
http://www.mckinsey.com/business-functions/business-technology/our-insights/big-data-the-next-frontier-for-innovation

Pigato, J. Entrepreneur: *How 9 Successful Companies Keep Their Customers,* Apr. 2015
https://www.entrepreneur.com/article/243764

Taleb N. *Fooled by Randomness: The Hidden Role of Chance in Life and in the Markets,* Random House Trade Paperbacks, 2005

Rush, K. *Meet the Obama Campaign's $250 Million Fundraising Platform,* Nov. 2012
http://kylerush.net/blog/meet-the-obama-campaigns-250-million-fundraising-platform/

Yu D. & Fleming J. *How Customers Interact With Their Banks,* Gallup, 2013
http://www.gallup.com/businessjournal/162107/customers-interact-banks.aspx

Dixon, M. et al. *The Effortless Experience: Conquering the New Battleground for Customer Loyalty,* Your Coach in a Box, Mar. 2014

Ragsdale, J. *The State of Unassisted Support 2014. Deflection Back on the Table; Self-Service Success Rates Rising,* June 2014
http://cdn.swcdn.net/creative/pdf/Whitepapers/SW-WP-The-State-of-Unassisted-Support-2014.pdf

McGovern, G. *Web Self-Service Management Principles and Business Case,* June 2014
http://www.customercarewords.com/webinars/web-self-service-management-principles-business-case.pdf

14
IDENTIFYING CUSTOMER
TOP TASKS

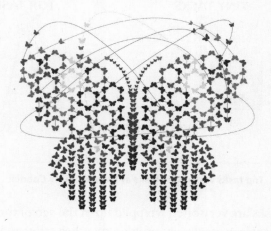

Identifying Customer Top Tasks
Top tasks versus tiny tasks

When we got citizens of Liverpool to vote on what they wanted from Liverpool City Council, we found top tasks such as libraries, leisure facilities, roads, waste collection. When we analyzed the relationship between publishing activities for the council on its website and citizens' top tasks, we found an inverse relationship. The more important the task was to the citizen, the less was being published on it, the less important it was to the citizen, the more that was being published on it.

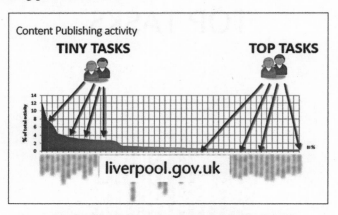

Top tasks versus tiny tasks at Liverpool City Council

The tiny tasks are very often wrapped up in the ego of the organization. They include: senior management profiles, speeches, news and press releases, annual reports, and general information about the organization. You are in dangerous territory when you come up against the ego of the tiny tasks, so tread carefully. Never make it about your opinion or your thinking. Always use customer data. Most organizations are willing to change once a compelling case is made. When Liverpool got the data on what citizens really wanted, it made the changes to become much more citizen-centric as can be seen from the homepage on the following page.

Remember: when a tiny task goes to sleep at night, it dreams of being a top task! Tiny tasks have high energy and ambition, and there are so many of them. Left unchecked, they proliferate and clutter the search, navigation and content. Most web teams I've met are being nibbled to death by tiny tasks.

They don't have time to focus on what really matters—the top tasks—because the organization is so vanity prone, inward-looking and organization-centric.

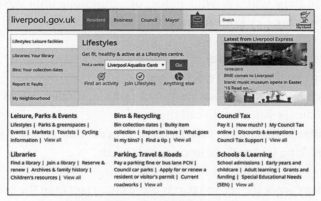

Liverpool City Council homepage

Steps in Top Tasks management

Top Tasks is a model of management that puts the customer at the center by measuring success based on the success of the customer at completing their top tasks. It involves the following steps:

1. Comprehensively engage the organization in a process of gathering customer tasks.
2. Work with key stakeholders to refine this initial list of tasks and come up with a final shortlist.
3. Get a representative sample of customers to vote, typically about 400.
4. Create a league table of tasks from the one with the highest vote to the one with the lowest vote.
5. Based on the results, select approximately the top 10 tasks and create very specific questions to test these tasks.
6. Use remote online, moderated testing, give these tasks to a representative sample of customers, and ask them to try and complete them. Record these sessions. Typically, you will need about 18 people.
7. Measure the success rate and the time on task. These become your key outcome-based metrics.
8. Carefully analyze the customer behavior and identify the core problems that are negatively impacting your metrics. Implement fixes for these

problems. Also look out for positive patterns of behavior that you could further encourage.

9. Use steps 6 to 8 as your model of continuous improvement, and as your core Key Performance Indicators.

Gathering customer tasks

There are two things you're doing here:

1. Collecting all relevant customer tasks, activities, micro moments—whatever you want to call them.
2. Initiating a change management process that gets key stakeholders thinking in detail about customer needs.

In many ways, the second part is more important than the first. Gathering the tasks becomes your excuse to talk to as wide a range of people as possible. It is vital you go out and start building bridges here. Every conversation you have is a potential for selling the need to be more customer-centric, for explaining the nature of the customer in the digital environment (impatient, skeptical, task-focused). You're sowing seeds here, preparing the ground for the task results—and the customer centric change—that will come later.

There are two essential sources for tasks:

1. The customer
   a. Surveys, research
   b. Support requests
   c. Social media, blogs, communities
   d. Search data both external search engines and from your own site
   e. Website / app data analysis: most popular sections, downloads, etc.
   f. A task collection survey that uses an open-ended question to ask people what their top three tasks are
2. The organization
   a. Corporate philosophy, strategy, mission, vision
   b. Stakeholder interviews and reviews
   c. Current website, app analysis
   d. Competitors / peers
   e. Industry media

The customer sources should always outweigh the organization sources. Always try and think from the world of the customer. If you are dealing with the subject of cancer, for example, collect the tasks from the perspective of the people who may have to deal with cancer. Be as complete as possible from their side, from their point of view. Your organization may not yet be dealing with tasks that are important to them, but it's important to find out from the broadest possible perspective what matters to them, rather than what your organization has or is capable of delivering right now. Remember, organize around the life of the customer.

Some say: Why go to so much bother? Why not just rely on search and site analytics? There are indeed circumstances where this approach can work, particularly where there is lots of historical data, and strong internal consensus on what the top tasks are, and more importantly, where there is very little pressure from tiny tasks. It really doesn't matter what method you use once you can:

1. Clearly identify the top tasks
2. Clearly identify the tiny tasks

Remember that search and site analytics do not always give the complete picture. Page visits reflect what you have, not necessarily what customers want. There may be tasks that you don't have content for—so it's unlikely they will show up in search and site data. And analysis of page views often reflects an amalgam of tasks; it's hard to separate the top tasks on these pages from the tiny tasks.

Search is a window into customer behavior, but it doesn't tell the whole story. For example, when we worked on the BBC intranet, we found they had a feature called "Top Searches" on their homepage. The problem was that once they published the top searches list, these terms no longer needed to be searched for, so in time a new list of top searches emerged!

When a website has a very bad navigation and information architecture, searches tend to be for top tasks because people depend on search more. However, when you have a very simple and well organized environment, search tends to be for exceptions. So, search results can be a mixed bag and need to be interpreted properly. Similarly, top tasks tend to get bookmarked, or people just go straight there out of habit, so such top tasks won't show up in search results.

Lots of people search for "remove conditional formatting" on the Excel section of the Microsoft website. Initially, Microsoft created a page explaining how to remove conditional formatting, but no matter how many times they revised the page, the satisfaction was always very low. After doing more extensive research, they discovered that the term "remove conditional formatting" was a symptom of the larger task of formatting in Excel. When they deleted the page on conditional formatting and sent people who search for "remove conditional formatting" to the overall page on how to format, satisfaction jumped. So, the words and terms that come up in search are not always a true reflection of the real task of the customer. Search is thus one input into the development of the customer task list.

Refining the tasks

A typical task gathering exercise for a large organization may collect between 300 and 500 tasks. When you're doing the collecting don't try too much to edit. Just make sure you've been as comprehensive as possible. Store the tasks in a spreadsheet.

What is a task? People assume that a task must always have a verb. But in a digital world where attention is at a premium, the less words—and the more specific these words are—the better. That means that you avoid verbs where possible. For example, do you really need "Find a Job" when you can just use "Jobs". You don't need "Get Pricing" when you can just use "Pricing". So, avoid verbs unless the verb is absolutely essential to the meaning of the task.

Your goal during this stage is to get this list of tasks below 100. In most of our task voting surveys, the final list is between 60 and 80. If possible take your time to do this. Typically, we allocate two weeks for gathering the tasks and four weeks for refining them. That's because:

1. We want to involve as wide a group of stakeholders in the process as possible.
2. It's very difficult to refine tasks properly in one go. We tend to have an average of two 2-hour shortlisting sessions a week (giving a total of about 6 sessions). This allows the list to settle but also allows stakeholders the time to go back to their groups and discuss specific issues that may have come up with a particular task.

You need to get a group together that will do the refining / shortlisting. This group typically has 3-8 people who represent the major stakeholders (Marketing, Sales, Support, IT, HR, etc.). The group should have experienced people who understand the organization and the customer. Otherwise, it will be very slow going as you attempt to reduce the size of the list. The group should be stable. If people are joining or leaving, then that really slows down the process. If there is an important stakeholder that you know is very busy, then involve them near the end of the process in an individual stakeholder review meeting.

The most obvious initial thing to do—which you can do on your own—is to get rid of exact duplicates and very strong overlaps. These will occur because you are compiling tasks from multiple sources. You want to avoid brand and product names, as well as tool and system names. Ignore tasks that are only for a specific audience or demographic. (Instead of "Treatment for women" use "Treatment".)

In researching a condition / disease what 5 factors are most important to you?				
Tasks	Overlap	Class	Source	Internal Source
Book your GP appointment online	appointment	Find services / experts	patients.co.uk	
Let me book an appointment	appointment	Find services / experts	user goals doc	
Make an appointment	appointment	Find services / experts	mayoclinic.com	
Remind me when it's time for my appointment	appointment	Living With	user goals doc	
Request an appointment	appointment	Find services / experts	netwellness	

Managing overlaps in task shortlisting

There's a lot of overlap in the tasks in the preceding table which needs to be cleaned up. At the end of the process, you'll probably end up with two tasks: Make an appointment; Appointment reminder. Or perhaps just one task: Appointments (make, remind)

As the shortlisting process nears an end, and the list is around 100, show it to key stakeholders for their feedback. The final list should be a consensus, but always make sure that it reflects the world and language of the customer. Sometimes, we allow a few tiny tasks from the organization into the list, just to show later that they get hardly any votes.

Getting customers to vote

Once you've got your final task list, you then need your customers to vote on this list. Let's say, for example, that you've a final list of 70 tasks. Let's say you put it together into a single question. You ask people to quickly scan the list and choose the 5 most important tasks to them. The question would look like this:

Crazy top tasks survey

I know that you're thinking that this is some sort of joke, right? I couldn't be serious, right? As crazy as it looks, it works. In the last 10 years, we have done over 400 similar surveys with close to 400,000 people voting.

There's method to the madness. This crazy survey is designed this way because we want to find out what really matters to people—what they do versus what they say they do. The very length and overload of the survey forces the gut instinct of the customer to kick in. You don't "read" the list; rather, you quickly scan it and the tasks that really matter to you jump out.

Using the results

The core purpose of the task identification survey is to clearly identify the top tasks and the tiny tasks. Every time we do this survey (and we have done it more than 400 times in 30 languages), we find similar patterns to what you see in the following pie chart for the OECD, an economic and policy advice organization.

The pie chart, on the following page, is broken up into quartiles of the vote. There were a total of 70 tasks that OECD customers were asked to vote on.

1. 4 tasks get the first 25%.
2. 6 tasks get the next 25%, so 10 tasks got the first 50% of the vote—the Top Tasks.
3. 11 tasks get from 50% to 75% of the vote.
4. 49 tasks get the final 25% of the vote—these are the tiny tasks. So, 4 tasks—top tasks—get as much of the vote as the bottom 49 tiny tasks. That gives a clarity of importance and focus.

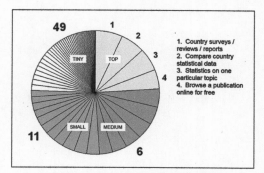

OECD customer top tasks results

We also ask organizational team / stakeholders to vote on a copy of the survey. When we did that with the OECD, here's what we got.

Tasks	Customer Vote%	Team Vote%	Empathy
Statistics on one particular topic	5.9%	9.6%	163%
Country surveys / reviews / reports	6.8%	5.4%	79%
Compare country statistical data	6.2%	5.2%	84%
Publication by topic	4.6%	5.1%	109%
Statistical forecasts / projections	3.8%	4.7%	124%
Overview of what OECD does	1.2%	4.7%	407%
Browse a publication online for free	5.1%	4.6%	91%
International guidelines and standards (corporate governance, tax havens, etc.)	3.2%	4.5%	141%
Basic facts, summaries and overviews	4.3%	4.0%	92%
Statistics on one particular country	4.0%	3.9%	98%

OECD stakeholders versus customer voting

We see that there is strong empathy and understanding between how the team and customer view the importance of tasks, with one exception. The team thinks "Overview of what the OECD does" is four times more important than the customer does. This method allows you to pinpoint with data where there are organizational blind spots, where the organization is out-of-sync with the customer.

You now have the vital data that allows you focus on what really matters to your customers—the top tasks. As we have seen, many organizations focus on launching more tiny tasks and over time that leads to a complex and overloaded digital environment where everybody loses. So, we now need to find out how well the top tasks are performing, and whether tiny tasks are indeed hurting the performance of top tasks.

15
CONTINUOUSLY IMPROVING
TOP TASKS

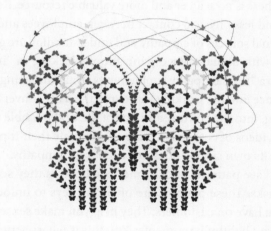

Continuously Improving Top Tasks
Task Performance Indicator

The Task Performance Indicator gives you a management metric that measures how easy and quick it is for your customers to perform their top tasks. It involves live remote observation of customers as they seek to complete their top tasks. It will give you defensible, trackable data, but often the most important thing it will give you is video evidence of real customers trying to carry out real tasks. You need to do this because:

a. You get to "see" your customers and thus you have the most valuable resource of all. The videos of your customers as they try—and often fail—to complete their tasks are the raw material of empathy. In a digital world, there is no scarcer and more valuable resource. Remember, there is less and less physical contact between employees and customers, so the normal sources of empathy and understanding are greatly reduced. It's like with digital your organization is lacking in "iron." You must take extra "iron" empathy supplements. You must bring the customers' experience into the working week, into the daily conversations, into the thinking, into the culture, and one of the best possible ways to do that is with videos of customer trying to complete their top tasks. Because data on its own simply does not encourage empathy.

b. You will see patterns of customer behavior as they seek to complete these tasks. These patterns are often the keys to unlock all the other data you have on customers. They help you make sense of all this data, giving you lightbulb moments: "Ah, this is what's actually happening. This makes sense now."

When we carry out a Task Performance Indicator, we spend most of our effort in observing the participants and seeking out key patterns of behavior. There are always patterns—typical ways that humans behave in a particular situation. One of your most important skills will be in identifying, communicating and acting on these patterns.

When we identify a major pattern of behavior that is causing task failure, we compile a video containing 3-6 customers who were affected. For each participant we select typically less than a minute's worth of video that illustrates the pattern. We then edit these 3-6 snippets into a combined video, which we try and keep under three minutes. Then we get as many stakeholders as possible to watch it. I have found that this is the single most powerful way to help the transformation from organization-centric to customer-centric. It has a particular potential to reach and influence senior management. You should seek to distribute these videos as widely and as often as possible. In an age of "digital touchpoints", that actually distance the organization from seeing their customers, these videos may be one of the rare times when a wide variety of employees will actually "see" the customer.

This is a management model

As we'll see in the next chapter on how Cisco uses the Task Performance Indicator, this is a customer experience model of management that focuses on customer outcomes. It gives you reliable and defensible data. You will be able to say things like: "This task has a 60% failure rate." If nothing is done to address the issues and you measure again in 6 months' time, it will still be a 60% failure rate. You are measuring customer outcomes as they seek to do what is most important to them, and these metrics are repeatable. This might sound simple and basic to you, but most organizations don't have reliable metrics to truly measure the customer experience.

The following chart shows why we can do this.

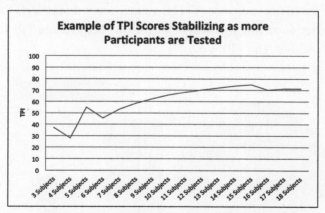

TPI score stabilization as more participants tested

In traditional usability testing, it has been long accepted that if you test with between 3 and 8 people, you will find out if there are significant problems.

This is true. But what you will not find out is what precise success rate and the time-on-task is involved. As a result of thousands of tests over many years, we have discovered that if you test with between 13 and 18 people, you will get reliable and stable patterns. (The makeup of the test participants should reflect the type of customers that are most important to your organization.)

Why is that so important? Because now you have a customer experience management metric. You can stand in front of management and say: "The Task Performance Indicator (TPI) score is 45. We have an average of a 40% failure rate for all tasks, and for those who are succeeding, it is taking them an average of 4 times longer than our target time." If nothing is done and you test again in 6 months, you will have pretty much the same figures to communicate. However, if you do make real improvements, you will be able to say something like: "The TPI is now 54. As a result of our efforts, the failure rate has dropped to 30%, and the time-on-task has been halved." Being able to say something like that is genuinely transformative. So few organizations have reliable management metrics that measure and track customer experience. Believe me, this can be a career-changing moment when management sees you as someone they must listen to because you've got the numbers.

How the Task Performance Indicator score is calculated

The Task Performance Indicator (TPI) is a single score that reflects the overall customer experience. The following chart shows the average TPI scores for a particular website. The TPI is 61.

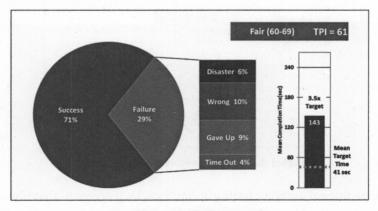

Overall task performance results

The TPI score is calculated based on the following elements:

1. If every task is successfully completed within the agreed target times, then the TPI will be 100.
2. Task failures reduce the TPI:
   a. A time out is where someone takes longer than the maximum time allocated. Most of the tasks we test have a target time of one minute or less. We set a maximum time limit of 5 minutes. If someone goes over that time, we mark the task as a Time Out.
   b. If someone says that they want to give up, then that is marked as a Give Up.
   c. If someone gives the wrong answer but if the answer is close to the right answer, and they express low confidence in their answer, then we mark it as a Wrong answer.
   d. If someone gives the wrong answer and acting on the information in that answer could have serious implications, and they express high confidence in their answer, we mark this as a Disaster. A Disaster will reduce the TPI significantly more than a Wrong answer will.
   e. When someone has low confidence even though they have got the correct answer, that has a slight negative impact on the TPI score.
   f. We set a target time for each task. The more above the target time someone is, the more it impacts the TPI score.

The following chart shows how the TPI was calculated for a particular organization. At 40, the TPI was not very good, and the chart shows what

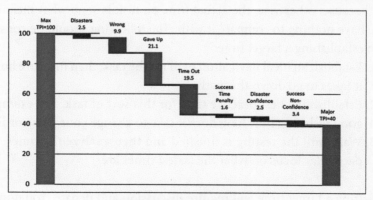

How the TPI is calculated

factors had the most impact on reducing the TPI.

What pulled down the TPI most in the preceding example was people giving up, timing out, and getting the answer wrong. A Success Non-Confidence penalty occurs when people get the right answer but state that they are not confident in it. A Disaster Confidence is where people have got a seriously wrong answer and they are completely confident about it. This has a significant impact on the TPI when it happens. A Success Time Penalty is where they get the right answer but take significantly longer than the target time.

We have developed a rating scale to understand the relative importance of a TPI score. Anything less than 35 is considered critical. In other words, you are giving the customer a horrible customer experience. A TPI of 80 or more is shows that you are delivering an excellent customer experience.

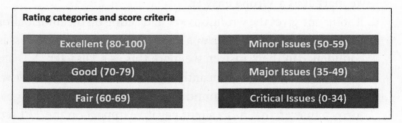

Rating categories and score criteria

Measuring time

In measuring time, we need to start off by establishing what we call the "Target Time." We must estimate how long it should take to complete a particular task, because, otherwise, the actual time on task is somewhat meaningless as we have nothing to compare it with. The following should be considered when establishing a target time:

1. Establish an ideal navigation path for the task, then measure how long it takes to go down this path.
2. Establish the best practice time for this sort of task. For example, on good websites, how long does it take to change your password?
3. Wait until the testing is finished and then analyze the times, with a particular focus on what the fastest times are.

Setting a target time will require discussion and debate. You don't have to be absolutely precise. We tend to work in blocks of 5 seconds (40, 45, 50 seconds), because it's only when the participant is taking twice or longer than the target time that the TPI score begins to get seriously affected. This brings us to the question of how should time affect the TPI. The following chart shows how we deal with it.

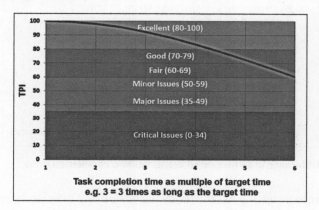

How time penalties are calculated

As you can see for the line running across and curving down the chart, the TPI doesn't reduce very much if the actual time is just twice the target time. An actual time that is 6 times higher than the target time reduces the TPI by 40 points. So, if everyone completed a particular task but they took 6 times the target time to complete it, then the TPI would be 60.

Benefits of remote testing

We have found remote testing, where you observe and record the person's screen and listen to them using a screen sharing tool, is both faster, cheaper and better than traditional lab-based measurement. The key point here is that you observe them in a live setting. In unmoderated remote testing, it is very difficult to ascertain whether someone has successfully completed the task or not, and that is a major disadvantage from a design and continuous improvement point of view. In a 2015 study, Measuring Usability found that while 93% of participants said they had completed a set of tasks successfully, only 33% of these tasks were verified as being actual successes. "The gulf between actual and reported behavior is the topic of many studies in the behavioral sciences, user research and that's also the case here. It's no wonder it's a cliché to 'watch what users do and not what they say.'"

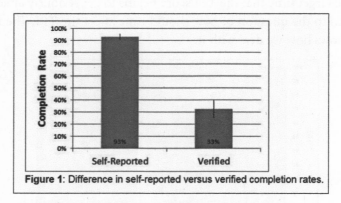

Figure 1: Difference in self-reported versus verified completion rates.

Difference in self-reported versus verified completion rates

Moderated, remote testing has the following advantages over lab-based testing:

1. **Faster:** You can set up tests much more quickly and more often. It's a lot easier for someone to give you 1 hour of their time online than for them to spend a morning visiting your lab. Because of this, remote testing can become part of the work-week, not something that is done occasionally. That's a transformative advantage because it allows you to make customer measurement an inherent part of the work week.

2. **Cheaper:** The cost of setting up a remote test is much lower than setting up a lab-based test. For remote, you don't have all the costs of a lab, for starters. For a lab-based test, a participant needs to travel. A one hour test can take up their morning. This makes it significantly harder to get participants and you will need to pay them more.

3. **Better:** "Now, please sit down at this computer that's not yours. And don't mind me and all my facial expressions as I sit beside you with my notepad. And forget about that camera that is broadcasting your every move to the web team in the next room. And ignore these strong lights and unfamiliar surroundings. Now, what I'd like you to do is imagine you're at home using your own computer and that I'm not here." You get better, more real and more natural behavior if the person is actually at home or in their own office, using their own computer with nobody

sitting beside them with a notepad. As a result, you will get better, more reliable and accurate task metrics and this is absolutely vital in building your new customer experience metrics.

Task questions

Remote testing removes a lot of the "noise" that is likely present during lab based testing. However, the one piece of "noise" that impacts most the likelihood of the participant behaving in a normal, natural way, is the task question itself. In choosing a task question, keep in mind the following:

1. **Based on customer top tasks:** You must choose task questions that are examples of top tasks. If you measure and then seek to improve the performance of tiny tasks, you may actually be contributing to a decline in the overall customer experience.

2. **Repeatable:** Create task questions that have a longevity to them and that you can measure roughly every six months. This means you have a management model for continuously improving the customer experience, not just a once-off series of tests.

3. **Representative & typical—fix it, fix many:** Don't make the task questions particularly difficult. For example, choose questions for one of your most popular products or services, not something unusual that has special exceptions. Then, when you identify and fix the problems brought up by the testing, you'll be fixing the problems for many other similar products.

4. **Universal—everyone can do it:** Every one of your test participants must be able to do each task, so don't choose a task question that only a sales person can do if you're going to be testing a mixture of technical, marketing and sales people.

5. **One task, one unique answer:** Each task question must only have one actual thing you want them to do and one unique answer. Remember, the more specific the task is, the better.

6. **Does not contain clues:** The task question is noise. The participant will examine it like Sherlock Holmes would a clue. So, try and make sure that it doesn't contain any obvious keywords that when searched with would lead directly to the answer.

7. Emotionally neutral, not confidential: Create boring task questions; nothing funny, witty or emotional about them. Avoid asking for any confidential information from the participant, as this may make them uneasy and thus less likely to perform in a natural manner.

8. Independent from other tasks: Don't have a sequence in the task questions. You shouldn't have to complete task 4 in order to be able to do task 5. This is because we likely to change the order we ask the questions in because if you keep asking the questions in the same order, there is a chance that the later questions will perform better because the person has got used to finding their way around the site.

9. Clearly different from other tasks: Don't ask the same type of task question twice. Otherwise, the person will learn something from the first task attempt and be likely to artificially do better at the second one.

10. Immediately doable: Task questions should be immediately doable on the website or app. You shouldn't have to sign up, for example, and wait for an email confirmation.

11. Short – 30 words or less: Remember, the participant is seeing each task question for the first time, so aim for a question that is ideally less than 20 words, and definitely less than 30 words. Otherwise, they're liable to forget what they have been asked halfway through the task.

12. Doable within 2 minutes maximum: Remote testing is not really suitable for long, complex tasks. So, we aim for tasks that have a target time of no more than one minute, and definitely no more than 2 minutes.

13. No change within testing period: Choose questions where the content or app is not likely to change significantly during the testing period. Otherwise, you're not going to be testing the same environment.

Top Tasks for OECD customers included the following:
1. Country surveys / reviews / reports
2. Compare country statistical data
3. Statistics on one particular topic
4. Browse a publication online for free
5. Working papers

Here's a sample of task questions that were developed based on these top tasks:

1. What are the OECD's latest recommendations regarding Japan's health-care system?
2. In 2008, was Vietnam on the list of countries that received official development assistance?
3. Did more males per capita die of heart attacks in Canada than in France in 2004?
4. What is the latest average starting salary, in US Dollars, of a primary school teacher across OECD countries?
5. What is the title of Box 1.2 on page 73 of OECD Employment Outlook 2009?
6. Find the title of the latest working paper about improvements to New Zealand's tax system.

Continuously improving

The Task Performance Indicator is a formal management model that gives you reliable metrics on customer task performance. It should be carried out on 10-12 of your customers' top tasks on a 6 or 12 monthly basis in order to get an accurate measure of the state of the customer experience.

In your daily work, you should be using as wide a range of metrics as possible—from usage statistics to simplified usability testing with 3-5 people—to figure out that you are going in the right direction. When you get the data back from the TPI, take the big problems that are hurting the TPI score and focus on them. Just test around a specific page, link, form or piece of content, and make improvements there. Immerse yourself in the behavior every day if possible because that is the foundation stone of the new model—never ending, continuously improving.

References

Sauro, J. *How Reliable Are Self-Reported Task Completion Rates?* Dec. 2015
http://www.measuringu.com/blog/self-reported-rates.php

16
TOP TASKS MANAGEMENT
@ CISCO

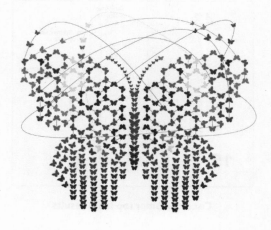

Top Tasks Management @ Cisco
From uploading software to helping customers download
The top tasks of Cisco customers are:
1. Downloading software
2. Configuration / set-up
3. Troubleshooting

Out of a final list of 67 tasks that customers voted on, these top three tasks got as much of the vote as the bottom 43. Since 2010, we have been running Task Performance Indicators, roughly every six months, to measure the performance of these tasks.

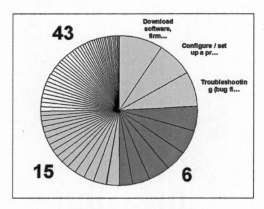

Cisco customer top tasks results

In 2010, when we started measuring software downloads, it could take a typical customer up to 15 steps and more than 300 seconds to download a piece of software. By 2012, for a significant percentage of software that had been reduced to an average of 4 steps and 40 seconds.

The key to the improvements was a change in culture and focus. It used to be that those involved in producing Cisco software felt that their job was done when they had uploaded the latest version onto the website. Now, they are focused on ensuring that customers can quickly and easily download the software. It's a classic shift from old-model, input-based organization-centric thinking, to new-model, outcome-based customer experience measurements. Success is measured not based on what Cisco does, but rather on what the customer achieves. We move from measuring what we produce to customer use.

According to Bill Skeet, Senior Manager of Customer Experience for Cisco Digital Support, this has had a "dramatic" impact on how people think about their jobs. "We now track the score of each task and set goals for each task. We have assigned tasks and goals to product managers to make sure we have a person responsible for managing the quality of the experience."

Once employees become focused on customer outcomes, their whole way of thinking and working changes. They get clear evidence on what is slowing down customers, what is complicating things, where they are getting lost, where they give up. For example, one of the software download tasks was:

Get to the download page for the latest release of software for Cisco's 7920 Wireless IP Phone.

The following image shows Step 7 in the original process.

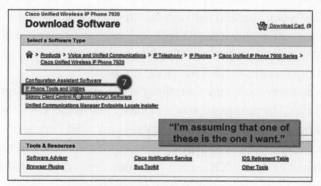

Download software webpage

The link that customers were supposed to click on was "IP Phone and Utilities". A clear pattern emerged when people arrived at this page. They were confused and didn't know which link to click on. The cursor kept moving back and forth, up and down, sometimes it would literally go around in circles. Sometimes it would stop dead still and then after several seconds, begin to tentatively move again. A typical comment from a customer was: "I'm assuming that one of these is the one I want." It is often simple changes to links that have the most dramatic impact in improving task performance.

The Task Performance Indicator gives you the context the customer is in.

Most other metrics tell you what is happening. TPI tells you why something is happening. You know what task they are trying to complete and that can really change your whole perspective. Jeffrey Davis, User Research Lead for Cisco, believes that there are two core questions for anyone working online:

1. What are your users trying to do? (NOT the same as what they are actually doing)
2. How well are they able to do what they are trying to do?

"It is vitally important to make the distinction between 'what users do (i.e. click on)' and 'what they are trying to do,'" Jeffrey states. "In talking to stakeholders, they often list web metric data as synonymous with 'what users are trying to do' (if they have any data at all). That is a dangerous position since it assumes that all users are accomplishing what they set out to do in the first place. The beauty of Top Tasks is that it measures what users ACTUALLY are trying to accomplish and also whether they are able to be successful in those tasks. When you add the visceral experience of a stakeholder actually watching user after user struggle with key tasks and score it with numerical values, that's a great research methodology that can really promote change within an organization—as it has done at Cisco."

The worst way to design something is to have 5 smart people in a room drinking lattes. The next worst way is to have 15 customers in a room drinking lattes, telling you what they think they do and what they want. "Decisions in the past were driven primarily by what customers said and not what they did," Bill Skeet explains. "Of course, that sometimes didn't yield great results because what users say and what they do can be quite different."

Fixing bugs and being in control

The Task Performance Indicator score is something you can control. If you don't do anything about a particular task, the score will remain the same the next time you measure. However, if you make improvements, the success rate will increase. The following image shows a series of scores received by the bug fix task:

> **Ports 2 and 3 on your ASR 9001 router, running v4.3.0 software, intermittently stop functioning for no apparent reason. Find the Cisco recommended fix or workaround for this issue.**

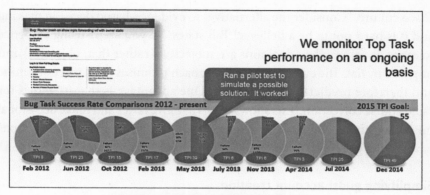

Performance of bug fix task: 2012-2014

For a variety of reasons, it was difficult to solve the underlying problems connected with finding the right bug fix information on the Cisco website. Thus, the scores from February 2012 to February 2013 did not improve in any significant way. For the May 2013 measurement, the team ran a pilot to show how, with the proper investment, it could be made a lot easier to find bug fix information. As we can see in the preceding image, the TPI jumped. However, it was only a pilot and by the next measurement, the TPI dropped again. The evidence was there though, and the team now got the resources to work on a permanent fix. The initial implementation was for the July 2014 measurement, where we see a significant improvement. More refinement was done, and by December 2014, the TPI was showing a major turnaround.

The Task Performance Indicator puts you in control of your own destiny, unlike other traditional customer satisfaction metrics. "We were driving the site experience by measuring 'customer satisfaction' with a monthly survey," Bill Skeet explains. "This metric was a lagging indicator at best. It was very difficult to see the effect of our changes in that metric as customer 'satisfaction' is a reflection of a conglomeration of experiences."

Being able to impact such a general metric as "customer satisfaction" has long been a challenge for organizations. If there's a price increase, for example, then customers may well be dissatisfied even though they've had a perfectly good support experience. If you ask about satisfaction on a Monday, you can get worse scores than if you ask on a Friday. Customer satisfaction metrics have also been found to be a poor indicator of customer behavior.

Evidence-based decision making is something that very much suits the

Cisco culture. "Consider the alternatives to evidence-based decision making and it is hard not to be a believer," Bill states. "If you aren't using evidence to make decisions, then decisions are subjective (rather than objective) and imposed by fiat. The evidence-based approach promises to be more scientific and therefore predictable and reliable. One advantage is that it "allows for rapid course correction. This allows teams to move faster and make occasional mistakes without long-term consequences. Unfortunately, many organizations have a history of executing monolithic projects in a 'launch and leave' fashion."

Simplifying guest account creation
When the following task was initially measured, the results were not good:
Create a new guest account to access the Cisco.com website and log in with this new account.

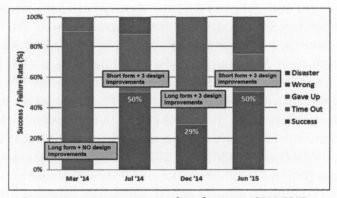

Create a new guest account task performance: 2014-2015

In fact, during the March 2014 measurements, nobody succeeded in completing the task. After the March measurements, three specific design improvements were made. These involved:
1. Clearly labelling mandatory fields
2. Improving password guidance
3. Eliminating address mismatch errors

As well, a shorter pilot form was launched as a test. In the July 2014 measurements, success jumped by 50%! However, by the December 2014 measurements, the pilot form was no longer there, and success dropped by 21%. By the June 2015 measurement, the shorter, simpler form was fully implemented, and success had again reached 50%.

The team was able to show that:

1. The three design improvements improved the success rate by 29%
2. The shorter form improved the success rate by 21%

That's very powerful. You can isolate a piece of work that you have done and link it to a specific increase in the TPI. You can start predicting that if we invest X, we will get a Y TPI increase. This is control and the route to power and respect within the organization.

And if you can link it with other Key Performance Indicators, then that's even more powerful. The following table shows that support requests

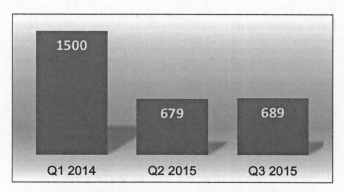

Create a new guest account support requests: 2014-2015

connected with guest account registration more than halved as a result of the improvements made to the registration form.

A more simplified guest registration process resulted in:

- 80% productivity improvement
- Registration time down to 2 minutes from 3:25
- 3 people less required to support customer registration

At every step of the way, the Task Performance Indicator gives you evidence which can be used against the voluminous opinion, which tends to exist within large organizations. For Jeanne Quinn, senior manager responsible for the

Cisco Partner website, "It's really helped us fight against some of the 'bright shiny object' disease and the tendency for everyone to have an opinion of what we put on our webpages—and where/how—because we have data to back it up. Our customers and partners do this—and not that—and when we organize content this way, they struggle, and when we organize it that way, they succeed! Clear and simple. Not easy to do mind you, but a fact-based approach that wins over colleagues and executives alike every time, and clears the way for us to make significant changes, and prove whether or not they are working for the most important folks—our partners."

Never-ending continuous improvement

When we measured the ability of customers to change their passwords, we found that 37% of them were failing. A process of improvement was undertaken, as can be seen by the following chart, and by December 2013, we had a 100% success rate.

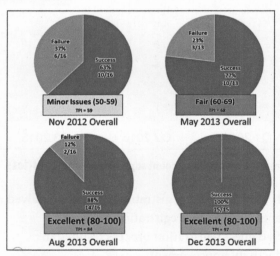

Changing passwords task performance: 2012-2013

100% success rate is a fantastic result. Job done, right? Wrong. In digital, the job is never done. It is always an evolving environment. You must keep measuring the top tasks because the digital environment that they exist within is constantly changing. Stuff is getting added, stuff is getting removed, and stuff just breaks.

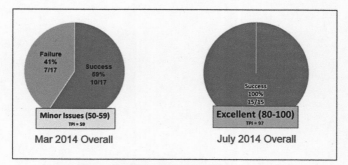

Changing passwords task performance: 2014

When we measured again in March 2014, the success rate had dropped to 59% because of a technical glitch. The glitch was quickly fixed and in July, it was back up to 100%. It never ends. That's digital transformation: from projects to processes, from organizational inputs to customer outcomes. A relentless focus on improving the customer experience by making it easier and faster for them to complete their top tasks.

17
SWITCH

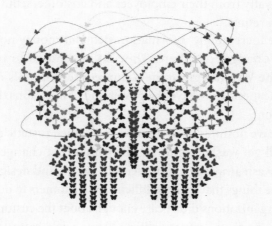

Switch

Switch. Switch jobs. Switch brands. Create open, simple, switchable designs. This is a time of great unpredictability and rapid change. You must be flexible and adaptable, skeptical, yet optimistic. Think open. Think transparent.

The old model is slowly collapsing. The "establishment"—the organization, the elites, the experts—are coming under increasing scrutiny. Wealth is concentrating in ever greater quantities in the top 1%, as the middle class is getting poorer, and those on low income struggle more and more every day. Societal contracts have been ripped up, mainly by brands and organizations, who expect loyalty from their employees and customers, but show precious little loyalty in return.

People are increasingly information rich and money poor. As a result, there is a lot of anger out there. They do not intend to remain passive bystanders. The Web has given them unprecedented tools of organization and communication. They have the power and connections that they simply never had before.

Switch. Leave nothing static because that which is static or slow moving or hidden will get washed away in this tsunami of change. The best way you can help wash away the old model is to switch and design the switches. Sometimes, the things that make it difficult for customers to do things are that way because organizations didn't care enough about the customer experience. But sometimes the complexity and difficulty was a deliberate part of the design and business model. Content was made deliberately complex and jargon-filled so as to confuse and frustrate. Unnecessary and time-consuming steps were added to a process in order to lock-in the customer, or to make them simply accept what's on offer. The old model didn't want you to think too much. It just wanted you to buy, to accept, to acquiesce.

The old model is a parasite on our lack of information, ignorance and laziness. It depends on us not thinking, not questioning and certainly not acting. So, if you want to do your part to usher in the new model and a fairer more transparent world, then you must switch as much as possible. I know that it's hassle. It took me years to switch my insurance companies, and I'm still in the process of switching my bank accounts. It's not easy. It takes time.

But if we all switch, think of what it will do. It will totally expose those who are ripping us off, because a foundation of the old model is the exploitation of loyal customers. By facilitating switching you will facilitate openness and transparency. The greatest strength for your organization will be that you have absolutely nothing to hide. Think if you could design something that allowed people to more easily compare, that allowed people to more easily understand. Think of how powerful that would be. That would build trust. That would build credibility. That would build brand. That would ensure longevity because you and your organization would remain fit. You would be strong and flexible because you would always be focused on what is best for the customer.

If you choose what is best for the organization—and that is by far the easiest option—then you choose a rapid route to extinction. Because your weakness will be your complexity—the locks and walls you have built—and once customers get an option to move, they will. Because—be guaranteed—your customers will find out that there is something better out there. Because—be guaranteed—your competitors will be doing their very best to make switching to them as easy as possible.

Switch to survive. Switch to thrive. The switch economy is already here. The compare economy is here. What I'm advising you to do is to stay up with the new model trends and build up your skill sets and experience around creating environments that empower customers, making their lives simpler and faster. Think fairness. Is this fair for the customer? Does it makes sense for customers to be loyal to us? Be on the side of your customers because your future career is in trouble if you stay with an organization whose business model is based on ignorance and blind loyalty.

Giving employees and customers control will be impossible for many organizations—and these will surely go extinct. Even the best organizations will constantly struggle with the idea that the customer should be given more control, so make sure that you keep your organization lean and customer-focused. And if you don't feel the organization you're with right now is truly capable of new model thinking, then switch jobs.

Putting the customer first means you must develop a deep, deep understanding of what matters most to them. This is an age of everything overload. There is massive abundance and glut out there, and everything is growing at a phenomenal pace. You must therefore have a clinical understanding of the top tasks of your customers. You must have that laser sharp focus of what's most important to them in any particular situation. Clutter—tiny tasks—kills the customer experience. Tiny tasks lie in a bed or organizational ego dreaming of being top tasks. They are the number one weed—the number one destroyer of the customer experience. You must eradicate them before they kill your design—and your career. Because it takes very little talent to design for tiny tasks. Anyone can add. It's the essence of the new model skillset to refine, to take away. The top tasks identification method that I have detailed in this book will give you a league table of what is most important—and least important to your customers.

The way you refine—the way you learn what to take away—is to get your design and content into the customers' world as quickly as possible. Design for use through use. Get your stuff used. See what is being used and make it simpler and simpler to use. The stuff that isn't being used, take it away. Are there gaps? Are there top tasks that you missed? They will emerge through use, through constant observation and feedback from customers. You'll see what missing as they give up in frustration, as they waste their time, as they suggest an improvement.

Measure success based on customer success. Use the Task Performance Indicator to figure out how easy and fast it is for your customers to complete their top tasks. Make changes based on evidence that shows where your customers are having difficulties. Continuously test. Continuously improve. And always look for opportunities to make it easier for the customer to switch, easier for the customer to compare, easier for the customer to understand. Because if you are loyal to your customers—if you genuinely seek to create the best possible customer experience for them—then they are far more likely to be loyal to you.

In order to transform your organization from tribal silos to a customer-centric network, you must flood it with the experience of your customers as they seek to complete their top tasks. The more the organization is exposed to the actual experience of customers, the more likely it is to develop empathy for customers—a prerequisite for creating an environment for the development of simple, fast customer-centric products and services.

Empathy is not enough, though. You must link the experiences of customers with the bottom line—wherever or whatever that is. You must link the experiences of customers with the key performance indicators of the organization. For many trained in old model thinking, it will seem counter-intuitive that what is good for the customer is good for the organization. Have no doubt, in this age of the customer, the link and the new logic exists—but it has to be shown and proven.

It won't be easy. It will be risky. You will often be seen as a troublemaker. You must remain nimble, flexible, and, above all, optimistic. The future is in your hands. The future is up to you.

INDEX